The Mechanics of Receiving Spirit Communications

STEPHEN A. HERMANN

Atendriya Press
Amherst, Massachusetts

Stephen A. Hermann/Atendriya Press
www.stevehermannmedium.com

Ordering Information:
Quantity sales. Special discounts are available on quantity purchases by corporations, associations, and others. For details, contact the "Special Sales Department" at the web address above.

Mediumship Mastery/ Stephen A Hermann. —1st ed.
ISBN-13 978-0692396087
ISBN-10: 069239608X

Table of Contents

This book is dedicated to my wonderful daughters Sadhana Bhakti, Radhe Shyam, Nitya Priya and Vedavati Emily.

The living entities in this conditioned world are My eternal fragmental parts. Due to conditioned life, they are struggling very hard with the six senses, which include the mind.

The living entity in the material world carries his different conceptions of life from one body to another as the air carries aromas. Thus he takes one kind of body and again quits it to take another.

The living entity, thus taking another gross body, obtains a certain type of ear, eye, tongue, nose and sense of touch, which are grouped about the mind. He thus enjoys a particular set of sense objects.

The foolish cannot understand how a living entity can quit his body, nor can they understand what sort of body he enjoys under the spell of the modes of nature. But one whose eyes are trained in knowledge can see all this.

—Bhagavad Gita 15.7-15.10

INTRODUCTION

I have learned much about human psychology in the many years that I have worked as a medium. After death we take with us the issues and defects of character that we fail to resolve or rectify in our physical lives. I often joke that if we need fifty years of psychotherapy and do not receive it while we are in the physical world that the healers and therapists in the spirit world will have their hands full.

Mediumship as a skill is an approach to impart higher direction to people in both dimensions. As I detail in this book, spirit communication enriches and improves the lives of people. The practice of spiritual mediumship brings forth proof of life after death and provides higher guidance and healing. Mediumship is not about fortune-telling or predicting the future, but operates on a far deeper level for the purpose of helping us understand our true nature as eternal spirit and our relationship to God. Mediumship is universal and forms the basis of many of the world's religions.

Mediumship is not something that is supernatural or extraordinary. Everyone is psychic and to some extent possesses mediumistic abilities. It is for this reason that I have always disliked the tendency for some mediums to place themselves on a pedestal above others as though their mediumistic development makes them special or distinct from others.

Mediumship rightfully has been compared to an artistic or musical talent. We all possess such skills, but proper training in a structured educational environment, facilitated by qualified instructors, will bring it out of us. So much of the technical skill required to produce representational art involves hand and eye coordination. But with patience, perseverance and proper tutoring in a classroom situation, an individual only able to draw stick figures would certainly, over a period of time, develop greater technical skill. It is the same with mediumship. A total novice can develop mediumship with the right training and personal effort. This book explores the mechanics of mediumship in an easy to read and practical way. It also examines the spiritual values necessary for higher levels of spirit communication. Mediumship skills are natural and may be cultivated and enhanced by anyone with the desire to do so.

Many individuals fear death and the unknown and feel uncomfortable with the subject of mediumship. The mere thought of communicating with the deceased on their own brings chills up their spines. It may seem incredibly fascinating to watch a television medium bring through deceased loved ones in the privacy of ones own living room, but observing another party do it is different from doing it yourself. There is nothing scary about communicating with the spirit world, unless we believe that it is scary. We all have mediumistic ability and when we get in touch with it, and understand how it operates, it can enrich our lives as well as those around us.

The untrained person, not knowledgeable about the mechanics and natural laws that make the process work may ask "What if you open up to dark spirits or negative entities?" Hollywood movies and sensationalistic television programs generally depict mediums as either mystical freaks or con-artists, and anything dealing with the spirit world is portrayed as frightening and potentially dangerous.

In addition, many denominations of Christianity teach against spirit communication even though both the Old and New Testaments contain numerous references to mediumship and various psychic phenomena, a fact ignored by many mainstream Christians. "Do not turn to mediums or seek out spiritists, for you will be defiled by them." (Leviticus 19:31) is a passage often quoted by those against mediumship. However, Jesus was a medium as were Moses, Daniel and the other prophets. Indeed, the essence of Christianity is based on the materialization of Jesus, after his physical death by crucifixion, which demonstrated to his devotees the reality of eternal life.

Psychic phenomena or mediumship is not limited to Christianity as many of the world's religious traditions, ancient and contemporary, were founded by powerful prophets who received great inspiration, guidance and teachings directly from the spirit world. Mohammed, the founder of Islam, received divine teachings from the Arch-Angel Gabriel. Joseph Smith, who established the Church of Jesus Christ of Latter Day Saints in upstate New York, was similarly spiritually directed by the angel world. In 19th-century Persia, the mystic Bahá'u'lláh received higher revelations, which which formed the philosophical foundation of the Bahai Faith, through his mediumship.

The ancient Greeks consulted the Oracle of Delphi and it is one example that indicates that spirit communication has been universally practiced throughout history. In all cultures and in all parts of the world, there have always been mediums or individuals possessing the ability to receive communications from the spirit world. Indeed, regardless of location, indigenous cultures have always made use of traditional healers or mediums to function as intermediaries between the spiritual and physical worlds.

Yet, so often there is fear involved with psychic experiences due to the interpretation of those involved and their own insecurities. While I have had many Roman Catholic priests and clergy from many religions come to me for sessions, the average, well-meaning priest or minister only reinforces, within their ministry, the misconception that communicating with the spirit world is dangerous as *you don't know who or what you could open up to.* It is no wonder that the average person has grave reservations about communicating with the dead.

And yet the dead are not really dead, are they? Mediumship is a means for even a non-medium to experience meaningful communications from recognizable personalities in the spirit world, who, as I have discovered in my work as a medium, are often more alive than the people here in the physical world. In all my years of working as a medium, I have never experienced anything negative or that made me feel uncomfortable. My experience with mediumship has always been genuinely positive, loving, and comfortable. I have communicated with thousands of spirit personalities through my mediumship and all conveyed information for the spiritual evolution of the recipient. I know that some people who watch me work for the first time expect that I will spit up green slime, turn my head *180* degrees and levitate. I would freak out if something like this were to happen and I would not practice mediumship.

I hope to teach people how mediumship works and how it is properly developed. I want to present how mediumship is a wonderful way to bring love, spiritual enlightenment, and healing to the world. Mediumship is a means of helping spirits who are in human form in the physical world as well as in the spirit world. When loved ones communicate recognizable details about themselves to those close to them in the physical world, great healing takes place for the recipient of the message. Through mediumship the bereaved are able to receive proof that their deceased loved ones continue to exist after physical death.

Even Atheists, who believe that human life is merely a biological coincidence, and that life after death could not possibly exist, may reconsider their view. They believe that spirit communication is impossible and that those with mediumistic abilities area either a fraud or deluded. And yet, when they receive information that is brought to them and validated, even such hardened skeptics may change their perspective.

Mediumship is a natural function. It should always be done with reverence and for the purpose of serving God and helping others. I have experienced lives completely transformed for the better as a result of spirit communication.

Microwaveable Mediumship

Over the past several years many books were published and popular television shows broadcast depicting spirit communication. This resulted in a widespread surge of individuals interested in experiencing personal sessions with mediums but also others wanting to demonstrate their own mediumistic abilities. Unfortunately, many of the former lacked adequate education and training.

A young woman, who had never been to a mediumship class before, attended one of my open groups in Massachusetts, where I was living at the time. After the class she was very excited and expressed her interest in continuing training. Although she called to find out if the class was taking place the following week, she did not show up. I did not hear from her again and figured that she had changed her mind.

About two months later I read the latest issue of a regional *New Age* publication that contained a directory of metaphysical practitioners and healers. *Communicate with your Deceased Loved Ones,* the ad copy read. I did a double take as I recognized the photograph of the young woman who was advertising her services as a professional medium. The beginners class that she had attended of mine was the only mediumship class that she had attended in her whole life.

If I read a manual on dentistry and own a set of pliers am I qualified to practice dentistry? Would any sane person want me to tear their teeth out? Mediumship, like dentistry, requires quality training. Education is essential for reliable mediumship and the more that people realize this the better. There are no shortcuts when it comes to mediumship training.

Many people in this modern age want things instantly without having to do the work. Mediumship is not microwavable and without proper training the standard demonstrated will be extremely lacking in reliability. I certainly have encountered over the years many individuals who have gone to psychics or mediums and not had favorable experiences, generally due to the insufficient training on the part of the practitioner.

Besides detailing the mechanics of mental mediumship, this book provides sections emphasizing the importance of continuing education, self development, and ethical and moral development for the student and practicing medium. I also include personal examples of my experiences as a medium and my philosophy regarding the practice of spirit communication. Far more is involved to develop mediumship than being merely able to accurately receive and convey spirit messages. The ideal instrument for the spirit world should be healthy in body, mind and spirit. While imperfections may exist on a human level, I emphasis self-care and personal growth in order to be the best possible channel for the spirit world to work through. Ethics and the development of personal character, emotional health and physical fitness, and their relationship to the unfoldment and practice of mediumship are comprehensively examined.

I have written this book to help students, regardless of experience, become better instruments for the spirit world to work through. Regardless of how many years we have studied mediumship, we can always get better and go further with our abilities. The emphasis of this book is on the mechanics of mental mediumship and proper methods of unfoldment. I feel that such a book is long overdue for while there are many interesting volumes dealing with mediumship development, most address the mechanics of the process at a superficial level leaving the serious student without adequate instruction.

I have taught development programs worldwide for many years to students of diverse nationalities and cultures. In my travels, often, I have had to make use of translators in my presentations, but regardless of the languages spoken or cultural distinctions, I have found that the faculties of mediumship may be developed within the context of the right educational environment.

In the past four decades I have read thousands of books on psychic unfoldment and the scientific investigation of mediumship written by leading mediums and prominent psychical researchers. I have also had the opportunity to attend training programs and sessions with many of the worlds foremost mediums and participated as a research medium with scientific experiments on mediumship at the University of Virginia. As such, I hope to present mediumship as it is, without any unnecessary mystification or speculative theories. Mediumship is not fantasy or the product of our imagination, but deals with objective reality and scientific principles.

My first experience with spirit communication took place when I was about two and a half years old, when the father of my mother, who had passed over two decades before, appeared to me and requested me to tell my mother that he had come through. I still remember the incident vividly and it was the first of many psychic experiences involving mediumistic contact and out-of-body travel that led me to formally study mediumship within the context of the Spiritualist movement. I was fortunate to study meditation as a child and be exposed to alternative approaches to spirituality and healing.

I graduated from Hampshire College in Amherst, Massachusetts, where I studied fine art, and I immediately devoted most of my energy to development as a medium. I moved from Massachusetts, where I had grown up, to Washington, DC, where I began attending development classes at the Church of Two Worlds, a Spiritualist church located in the heart of the historic Georgetown section of the city. Besides the training programs at the church, I participated in development circles in the residences of several experienced mediums.

This intense study of spirit communication included my formal enrollment in a Spiritualist seminary in which I earned credentials as a certified medium, teacher, and ordained minister with the National Spiritualist Association of Churches, the oldest and largest Spiritualist organization in the United States. I also devoured every available text on the subject and participated in as many training programs as possible. In order to complement my education as a medium, I explored other healing modalities including an intensive two year program in massage therapy and a certification training for hypnotherapy. My social life was nonexistent as weekends and most evenings were devoted to my training. A few months before my ordination, I quite my office job and embarked on a career as a professional medium.

Unlike many mediums, who stay in one location, my work internationally as a medium has exposed me to many different approaches to developing the various phases of mediumship. I have studied and applied in training for my own students training methods that have enhanced their capabilities significantly. Over the years, I have seen many mediums of varying abilities work. While there are many genuine and reliable mediums practicing and teaching, due to a lack of sufficient education, delusion and fraud still run rampant within the field. Mediums have the responsibility to develop themselves spiritually.

In terms of training methods, there is not one right approach that works for everyone. Mediumship development is very personal and must be adjusted to accommodate the individual students propensities. A good teacher of mediumship will telepathically be directed by teachers in the spirit world to properly bring out the abilities of the particular student. Often teachers of mediumship will discourage their students from studying with other teachers or utilizing methods other than their own. But we all learn differently, don't we? It is the teachers duty to bring out the student abilities using whatever methods work.

This book explains how the various phases of mental mediumship operate and presents techniques and exercises that may be used to exercise the psychic muscle and strengthen the connection with the spirit world. I also provide sections for professional mediums engaged in private sessions, public demonstrations, and media appearances. Mediumship is all about cooperation and team work and when we do our part the spirit team who work with us are able to more efficiently do theirs.

About the Exercises

The exercises presented in this book are designed for teachers of mediumship and circle leaders to utilize in the context of mediumship development programs. Some of the exercises were created by me with inspiration from my spirit teachers, while others are my versions of popular exercises used by many teachers of mediumship. All of the exercises presented have been effectively applied by myself and my students. The exercises are appropriate for both novice and experienced students. It is suggested that modifications be made as necessary depending upon the specific needs and circumstances involving the particular students or groups.

CHAPTER 1

Awareness of Spirit

The Phenomena of Spiritualism consists of Prophecy, Clairvoyance, Clairaudience, Gift of Tongues, Laying on of Hands, Healing, Visions, Trance, Apports, Levitation, Raps, Automatic and Independent Writings and Paintings, Voice, Materialization, Photography, Psychometry and any other manifestation proving the continuity of life as demonstrated through the Physical and Spiritual senses and faculties of man.[1]

Mediumship within itself is not spiritual. It is a mistake to think that by cultivating clairvoyance or the ability to see personalities in the spirit world that one is spiritually advanced or developed. Spirituality is about our relationship with God and developing ourselves as individuals. Mediumship within itself may be used for high or low purposes. The motivation of the medium may be either completely selfish or spiritually altruistic. Development of mystic powers should never be an end unto itself. What matters is how one's mediumship is used.

Sometimes people refer to mediumship as a gift which is true in the sense that the higher love, wisdom and inspiration that may be imparted is a great spiritual blessing. Only the Divine may bestow such spiritual gifts, but the faculty is inherent within everyone. It is not supernatural or extraordinary, it is natural ability worth cultivating for the purpose of self-improvement and selfless service to God and the spirit world.

Mediumship is not a game or a cheap form of entertainment. Nobody should actively practice mediumship without proper training and reverence for what is taking place. One of the laws of mediumship is the Law of Attraction. *Like attracts like.* We attract similar minded personalities to us based on our spirituality and mentality. This applies equally to people who are energetically drawn into our lives in the physical world, but even more so to the types of personalities we attract from the spirit world.

If someone is drunk at a party at 3 AM and plays with a *Ouija* board for cheap kicks, what sort of individuals will they attract from the spirit world? Mediumship is a big responsibility and once we open the door to the spirit world we need to learn how to properly close it and work with whoever comes through. We need to learn to be in control of ourselves and to understand the mechanics of the process.

There is nothing worse than an undisciplined medium, who, like a leaky faucet, leaves himself or herself open to anyone wanting to communicate from the spirit world, at all times and all places. I knew a medium who would deliberately approach strangers in public places such as his dentist's waiting room or fast-food restaurants and deliver spirit messages to them. He is fortunate that he didn't get maced. There is a time and place for mediumship. Entertaining intoxicated people at a cocktail party or strangers at a shopping mall is not the right atmosphere nor is the motivation proper.

Spiritual mediumship is a carefully planned and orchestrated process facilitated by higher guides in the spirit world. Many psychics will utilize cards or other devices such as crystal balls in their readings. A medium receives his or her information directly from the spirit world. A psychic may provide some amazingly accurate predictions for those who consult them. There is nothing wrong with operating on a psychic level as it often leads to spiritual mediumship and clearly demonstrates that there is more to life than merely the physical.

While a medium is always psychic, a psychic is not necessarily a medium, the difference being the source of the information. Mediumistic information is conveyed by living personalities in the spirit world and psychic information is obtained from the energy fields or auras of those living in the physical or the energetic atmosphere of a physical location or material object.

Everyone is essentially a spiritual being, an eternal spirit soul temporarily functioning through a physical vehicle or body. The physical body is always changing from birth, through youth, middle-age and death and yet, the soul or consciousness within remains the same. It is a big illusion to believe that life is the result of the combination of chemicals or matter. Life comes from life and all life is of God. Many highly educated people do not believe in life after death or that mediumship is possible. Life is far more than merely the physical and this physical world is not our true home. It is like a motel that we temporarily inhabit only to be forced to vacate when our physical body ceases to function.

What is a medium? The National Spiritualist Association of Churches (USA) defines a medium as "...one whose organism is sensitive to vibrations from the spirit world and through whose instrumentality, intelligences in that world are able to convey messages and produce the phenomena of Spiritualism."[2] There are many types of mediumship, which may be categorized in two main phases: mental mediumship and physical mediumship.

Mental mediumship is subjective in nature as it involves the inner intuitive experience of the medium and is dependent upon attunement of the medium with the spirit personalities. The intellectual, emotional, and spiritual qualities of the medium affect the nature of the mediumship as the medium's mind is directly involved in the process. More mediums perform mental medumship as physical mediumship is less common.

Physical mediumship is completely objective in nature as the five physical senses directly experience the phenomena taking place. Unlike mental mediumship, physical mediumship is not dependent upon the spirituality, emotional or intellectual qualities of the medium, but instead is dependent upon the chemistry of the physical medium or the group of individuals involved in producing the phenomena.

Physical mediumship is rare and often involves the extraction of ectoplasm from the physical body of the medium and others involved in the session. Very few mediums possess the qualities sufficient to produce physical phenomena. Ectoplasm is utilized by the spirit personalities as a substance to produce physical manifestations that are experienced directly by the five physical senses. When physical phenomena takes place everyone physically present experiences the same thing in terms of witnessing the manifestations.

The following are phases of mediumship subdivided into the two categories:

Mental

Automatic Writing and Painting: The medium is controlled by the spirit personalities to produce writings or artistic works at great speed.

Clairaliance: Clear smelling. Psychically smelling.

Clairaudience: Clairaudience. Clear hearing. Psychically hearing.

Claircognizance: Clear knowing. Psychically knowing.

Clairgustance: Clear tasting. Psychically tasting.

Clairsentience: Clear sensing. Psychically sensing or feeling.

Clairvoyance: Clear seeing. Psychically seeing.

Gift of Tongues: The medium is mentally impressed or controlled to speak foreign or unknown languages.

Impersonation: The medium is overshadowed by the spirit personality and takes on the mannerisms, gestures, and voice patterns of the communicator.

Inspirational Speaking, Writing, Painting, Music, etc: The mental influence of ideas and feelings from the spirit world expressed through speaking, writing or various artistic or musical mediums.

Interpretation of Tongues: The ability to interpret the spirit messages given in unknown languages through the gift of tongues.

Psychic Art: Art produced through the mental influence and control of spirit personalities. Psychic art may received through inspiration, clairvoyance, claircognizance and clairsentience as well as through more direct control at rapid speeds as with automatic writing.

Psychometry: The ability to psychically read or discern information through the energy contained within a physical object about the past history and present conditions of individuals or events associated with the object.

Spiritual Healing Absent or Distant Treatments: Spiritual healing through prayer for recipients not physically present and at a distance from the healer.

Spiritual Healing Contact or Auric Treatment: Spiritual healing through prayer and the physical laying on of hands or positioning the hands within the energy fields of the recipient.

Trance or Automatic Speaking: Controlled speaking in which spirit personalities utilize the mediums vocal mechanism for conveying messages.

Physical

Apportation: The dematerialization of physical objects by the spirit chemists, which are teleported to another physical location where they are rematerialized to their original form.

Automatic Writing and Painting: The control of the medium to produce writing or works of art at great speeds. An ectoplasmic arm of the controlling spirit may materialize over the arm of the medium.

Direct Independent Writing and Painting: The production of writing or works of art through various mediums by the spirit personalities without any physical contact with the medium.

Etherealization: A partial or full materialized spirit form self-illuminated by an almost phosphorescent light.

Fire and Cold Tests: The handling of objects of extreme temperature by the medium while in an altered-state and controlled by the spirit personalities.

Independent and Direct Voice: Independent voice mediumship involves the creation of an ectoplasmic voice box to produce sounds by the spirit personalities. Direct voice takes place with a spirit trumpet that acts as a psychic megaphone to amplify and direct the communications.

Levitation: The movement of the medium or physical objects through spirit power.

Lumination: The production of light in a darkened room, in which the physical space is illuminated by the spirit power.

Materialization: The use of ectoplasm to create a partial or full form of spirit personalities.

The Planchette, *Ouija* Board or Similar Devices: The use of such physical tools for communication by spirit personalities while controlling the medium.

Raps: The production of rapping or percussion noises by the spirit personalities

Spirit Lights: The production of lights of various sizes and shapes by the spirit personalities in a darkened room.

Spiritual Healing Contact or Auric Treatment: The use of spirit energies to impart physical cures through prayer and the physical laying on of hands or positioning the hands within the energy fields of the recipient.

Spirit Photography: The use of photography to obtain images of spirit personalities and other effects.

Table Tilting/Tipping: The use of the table for spirit communication through movements to convey information.

Transfiguration: The use of ectoplasm to create a mask over the face of the medium that is molded to resemble the features of spirit personalities. A full ectoplasmic form may also be molded over the entire or partial body of the medium.

Writing on Skin: The production of messages or images on the skin of the medium by the spirit personalities.

Sadly, so much unnecessary emphasis is placed on the physical body without understanding the eternal nature of the soul. It is like taking care of a birdcage but neglecting the bird living inside. This false identification with matter and that which is impermanent is ultimately the source of all our problems and sorrows. While the development of mediumship differs from God realization, it never the less is a wonderful tool that enables the seeker of truth to experience in a practical manner that there is more to life than merely the mundane universe.

The physical body is perfectly designed for this corporal dimension. The five physical senses of seeing, hearing, tasting, smelling and touching enable the soul to interact and operate within the environment of the physical world. The type of physical body that a soul may inhabit is appropriate for its development of consciousness and physical environment. Various species of fish or aquatics are effectively able to live in an underwater environment. Taken out of the water they would perish. There are advantages and limitations with every type of physical body. This is especially true when it comes to the sense organs found within the various species. Dogs for example compared to human beings are able to hear sounds inaudible to the human ear and detect smells that the human nose would fail to discern.

Mediumship involves the utilization of the mind to register higher frequencies of nonphysical energies. Such energies cannot be detected through the use of mechanical, scientific devices or by the limited five physical senses. After the Law of Attraction the most important natural law relating to mediumship is the Law of Vibration, which states that everything in the universe is operating at a particular frequency of energy or vibration. Just because one cannot see certain colors or hear certain sounds does not mean that they are not there or do not exist.

Due to the advent of modern electronic technology, the space around us contains innumerable waves of various, unseen communications. Each radio or television channel operates on a different frequency of vibration. We cannot see or hear the information being transmitted *via* these mediums through our limited physical senses and yet with a television or radio the frequencies are properly receives, sorted out and played for our viewing or listening pleasure. Mental mediumship is dependent upon telepathic rapport between the medium and the communicating spirit. A trained medium through the practice of meditation and prayer is able to raise their own personal vibration and mentally connect to register and convey communications from the spirit personalities.

Everything is energy or vibration. The spirit world is not in some far off place, but is around us interpenetrating the space of the physical world. The master teacher Jesus said, "In my Father's house are many mansions," which means that there are many worlds, both physical and subtle, for the soul to possibly reside in. These subtle worlds are described within the scriptures and teachings of many religious traditions as well as communications received mediumistically from personalities in the spirit world. The rate of vibration is much quicker in the spirit world compared to the much denser atmosphere of the physical world. In order for communications to work the medium must raise his or her vibrations and the spirit personalities must lower theirs. This is one of the reasons why regular prayer and meditation are essential for mediums as they enable the medium to consciously raise his or her own vibration and better connect with the spirit world.

The Subtle Bodies

We possess several subtle bodies interpenetrating the physical body. Within the Chinese and other Oriental systems of healing are extensive details of the subtle anatomy and energetic systems. This is also especially true of the Yogic or Vedic system originating in ancient India, which incorporates awareness of the subtle bodies and energies in its spiritual and healing tradition.

Vedas is a *Sanskrit* word that originated in India and means knowledge. The Vedas are the oldest and most comprehensive religious and philosophical teachings known to man. According to the Vedas, the individual soul or consciousness is enveloped by several covers the densest of which is the physical body followed by the mind, intelligence, and false ego. The mind may be compared to a computer, the intelligence is the program and the false ego is the identification with a temporary role such as the belief that one is a particular gender, age, nationality or religion. These designations are temporary and are fully based upon the physical body. At the moment of physical death the soul leaves the physical body to reside in an appropriate environment in the spirit world. The soul's destination after physical death is determined by the development of its consciousness.

The Aura

The aura or energy fields that emanate around the physical body are extensions of these subtle bodies. The layers of the aura interpenetrate and reflect the nature of the individual. The densest layer of the aura is that closest to the physical body is related to the etheric body and reflects largely the physical health of the individual. The etheric body is an energetic body interpenetrating the physical body. It acts as a blueprint for the physical body and as such diseases and pathological conditions may be psychically detected often before they physically manifest.

The next layer of the aura relates to the emotional nature of the individual. Clairvoyantly, the emotional layer of the aura resembles a cloudlike formation of colors that reflect the emotions of the individual. There may be some colors that indicate the general temperament of the individual combined with others that change as the individuals moods shift.

The mental and intellectual layers of the aura extend past the emotional field and indicate much about the character and personality of the individual. Although there may be prominent colors present, there may be much activity in relation to the thought processes of the individual.

Lastly, is the largest layer of the aura known as the spiritual field, which extends the furthest from the physical body. Spiritually elevated individuals radiate a beautiful spiritual light that is strongly felt by those around them. Materialistically inclined individuals are like animals locked mainly into instinct and as such lack a developed spiritual aura.

The aura is entirely connected to the process of mental mediumship in that the spirit personalities work through the energy fields of the medium. When a medium opens up to work with the spirit world, the energy field surrounding her greatly expands. Understanding the nature of the aura and how it relates to the process of mediumship is essential and will be discussed in detail in successive chapters.

The Chakras

Chakra is a *Sanskrit* word meaning wheel. The chakras serve as a transmitter of life energies connecting the various bodies. Each of the major chakras relates to glands within the physical body as well as different phases of mediumship. A by-product of awakening or activating the energy centers is that the individual experiences or cultivates various psychic or mystical powers.

Within the Yogic tradition each chakra is associated with a specific color, sound vibration and other properties. It is beyond the scope of this book to elaborate upon this in detail, but the relationship of chakras to mediumship should be mentioned as such understanding directly relates to the development of psychic ability.

Major Chakras

Base of Spine. The main energy channels flow through the nervous system within the spinal column. This energy is used in all aspects of mediumship work.

Sexual Organs. Sexual energy is psychic energy. The natural reproductive energy in this area may be used to strengthen the medium physically and mentally. Energetically such life force properly controlled may be utilized for greater God realization and psychic potency.

Navel. Located two inches below the navel, this chakra controls all the functions of the physical body. In Asian martial arts this point generates internal power used for physical techniques. This same chakra helps mediums integrate with their physical bodies by balancing the tendency to mentally disassociate during periods when mediumship is not being done.

Solar Plexus. The spirit operators draw upon psychic force from this energy center, which additionally acts as an outlet for ectoplasm during the production of physical phenomena. Emotions and energies may also felt at this center through clairsentience.

Heart. An activated heart chakra radiates unconditional love and healing to those in need. The vibrations of this chakra also relate closely with levels of entrancement as well as emotional feelings that may be experienced through clairsentience.

Throat. The throat chakra relates to clairaudience or psychic hearing. Trance channeling also utilizes the throat chakra as does voice mediumship in which an ectoplasmic duplicate of the medium's voice box is created for the production of sound.

Forehead. This chakra is the location of the mystical third eye which when activated results in various types of clairvoyance or psychic vision.

Crown. The crown chakra located at the top of the head connects the soul to universal consciousness. It is through this chakra that the higher masters are able to impart greater, cosmic wisdom.

Minor Chakras on Hands and Feet. The chakras on the feet are used to take in energy from the earth as well as ground the medium during periods of rest from mediumship. The hand chakras are used to direct and focus healing energies during treatments by spirit doctors.

Reading Energy

A psychic is able to tune into information energetically present within the aura of the individual. The dynamics of a psychic reading are different than using psychic abilities to receive messages from spirit personalities. During a psychic reading the psychic feels as through he or she is mentally connecting with the recipient. Psychic impressions come by the way of images, feelings, smells, tastes, sounds or knowing. The energy involved in psychic reading is static and not alive or heightened as with mediumistic communication.

People read the aura all the time without even realizing what they are doing. Someone around us may be depressed or angry, without any visual cues, and we will be aware of exactly what they are feeling. We could be purchasing a car and sense and sense if the dealer is honest or dishonest from the energy emanating from him or her.

Telepathy

Telepathy, or thought transference, is common in the physical world especially if there is a strong emotional connection between the parties. How many times have the following examples taken place? The phone rings and you know exactly who is calling before you pick up the receiver? You think of a friend, whom you have not seen in a long time, only to physically run into him later that day? Telepathy is not limited by earthly distance as demonstrated by the mother, who feels that something is wrong with a daughter living at a distance, and upon phoning her discovers that her feelings were correct. Telepathy is the means by which personalities in the spirit world are able to impart their ideas and messages to us. Many people are influenced by the spirit world and do not even realize it.

Psychic Atmosphere

Psychic energy may also be experienced at various physical sites which reflect the nature of its occupants or events that have taken place at that location. The vibrations at a bar or night club are distinctly different than the energies present at a church or temple. Someone sufficiently sensitive could be taken blindfolded to either location and would accurately be aware of the energies present.

It is not uncommon for individuals sensitive to energy to psychically pick up on the vibrations of specific locations, perhaps where an emotionally charged event took place. Locations where much physical life was lost and great suffering has occurred such as battlefields, prisons, and psychiatric institutions may leave particularly strong negative energetic imprints. Such negative residual energy is not always easily cleared and may be experienced many years later.

Psychometry

Physical objects energetically contain a history of the events and people connected with the object. A piece of jewelry or personal item owned by an individual may be held by a sensitive to be accurately read on a psychic level. This type of psychic discernment is known as psychometry, which means *soul measure* or reading the history of physical objects. People practice psychometry all the time and are not even aware of what is taking place. They may receive a letter or card in the mail and know exactly what the contents of the correspondence are before opening it.

Once while visiting England, I visited an old manor house which was open as a museum. In one room were many artifacts dating back many centuries that had been used as torture devices to inflict pain on people. I did not have to physically touch or hold the objects to feel the ugly, horrible, dark energy present with them.

Psychometry is a good tool for developing mediums. I acquired several pieces of driftwood from a beach near where I was staying during my first trip as a medium to New Zealand. A few weeks later back in the States, I handed a plastic bag containing the driftwood to a friend of mine and asked her to hold it and describe what she psychically felt with it. She immediately, although untrained as a medium and not knowing the contents of the bag, accurately described the beach where I had found the driftwood.

Another time in New Zealand, a friend of mine handed me a document belonging to his family that dated back to the early 19th-century. I proceeded to describe in great detail the history of the object, all of which my friend validated. The document belonged to his ancestors who had been involved in the *Dutch East India Company.*

The practice of psychometry is exceptionally effective as a means of enhancing psychic ability as well as gaining confidence in psychic skill as a result of feedback provided by others. When I work with psychometry I generally do not work psychically but instead connect with the spirit world and receive messages for the owner of the object.

Many years ago, I had a mother and daughter from nearby Vermont attend a mediumship development class that I was teaching at my healing center in Massachusetts. The mother downplayed her abilities and considered herself lacking any psychic potential whatsoever. During the class I had the students each place a personal object in a basket. After the meditation period each student would pick an object belonging to someone else and read for the owner using psychometry or direct mediumship.

The mother was the last person in the class to do the exercise. After making excuses about how inferior her psychic skills were, she proceeded to read the object and concluded by stating that it belonged to the woman sitting next to her. It did indeed belong to the woman next to her, who could understand everything that the mother had stated in her reading. This just goes to show that often the people who think that they have the least ability may in reality possess the greatest amount of talent.

Telepathic Awareness Exercises

EXERCISE 1

Telepathy with Numbers

Participants pair up and face each other in chairs. After a short period of meditation one partner strongly thinks of and feels a number between one and ten, while the other attempts after a short time to telepathically tune in and pick up on the number. The more spontaneous the response the better. Multiple attempts may be practiced with one side before repeating the exercise with the other partner.

EXERCISE 2

Telepathy with Shapes

This exercise is the same as exercise 1, the only difference is that one participant strongly thinks of a shape with his or her partner attempting to telepathically tune in.

EXERCISE 3

Telepathy with Colors

This exercise is the same as exercise 1, the only difference is that one participant strongly thinks of a color with the partner attempting to telepathically tune in. The more vivid and intensely the participants visualize their color, the easier it will be for their partners to pick up on it.

EXERCISE 4

Sensing Emotions

One partner remains seated with the other standing behind. The seated partner goes back into the memories of his or her life and finds an incident that invokes a particularly strong emotion. The emotion might be the happiness associated with a wedding or the depression connected to the passing of a loved one. Participants should carefully select only a memory associated with an intense emotional response.

After spending a short period building up the memory and emotion associated with it intensely, the partner will approach him or her from behind and placing his or her hands upon the shoulders attempt to tune in as to the specific emotion. After sharing with each other and providing feedback the positions of the students is reversed and the exercised repeated.

EXERCISE 5

Contrasting Lower Thoughts With Higher Vibrations

Participants take partners with one seated while other stands at a distance. The participant sits in a meditative state and mentally recollects a particular incident in their life that made them extremely unhappy such as a divorce or passing of a close loved one.

Meanwhile the partner standing behind at a distance concentrates on filling the space around themselves with love and healing. The greater the distance between the partners the better.

At the signal of the teacher, the participant standing begins to slowly walk toward his or her seated partner all the time mentally sending love to him or her. The seated participant should raise his or her hand the moment he or she feels the love. Until this takes place the standing participant should continue slowly walking toward his or her partner and, if necessary, place his or her hands on gently on the shoulders. After giving feedback about their experience, the exercise may be repeated with partners reversing positions.

EXERCISE 6

Group Telepathy Colors

The teacher may divide, if necessary, a larger group into smaller groups of five to eight people. In each group, one participant will be selected to mentally visualize a color strongly and vividly around himself or herself. After a short period, the other members of the group will tune in telepathically and share what they feel the visualized color to be. Members may take turns at selecting a color and letting the others in the group tune in.

EXERCISE 7

Group Telepathy with Colors Projected

This is the same as exercise 6. But in in this case, the subject, after spending a short period intensely visualizing a chosen color, will attempt to mentally project this color to others in the group, who will attempt to tune in and share what they feel the color to be. This exercise may be repeated with others taking turns projecting a color. Some students will be better at mentally projecting, while others will be stronger at mentally receiving.

Auric Field Awareness Exercises

EXERCISE 8

Feeling Life Energy Between the Hands

Participants rub hands together and feel energy between palms and around their hands and fingers. Common sensations experienced by participants include increased temperature, tingling and feelings of magnetic pulling and pushing between the hands.

EXERCISE 9

Sensing Life Energies of Others

Continuing where exercise 8 left off, participants pair up facing each other with palms out and feeling same sensations with partners palms as done individually. Participants can share their experiences with each other as well as the rest of the group.

EXERCISE 10

Auric Sensing

This exercise ideally should be done in a large room or outside open space. Participants pair up with partners, who stand directly behind them at a distance. The further the away the better. At the signal, those standing behind slowly walk as silently as possible toward their partner.

As soon as participants feel the presence of their partners walking toward them they raise their hands and the partner immediately stops moving toward them. Until their partners raise their hand, participants should walk until they are standing directly behind their partners, without touching them.

Once all the partners doing the sensing have raised their hands, participants can turn around and notice the distance of their partner from them. Participants can switch roles and repeat the exercise.

EXERCISE 11

Seeing and Sensing the Aura

One participant sits or stands in front of the group with a dull or white backdrop. Participants attempt to objectively view the aura while keeping their eyes open and looking around and off to the side of the individual in front of them. Participants may also close their eyes and mentally tune into the subject and attempt to mentally see the colors as well as feel the energy.

Whatever feelings and impressions received as well as interpretations by participants should be shared either spontaneously or as requested by the instructor. The teacher should emphasis the interpenetrating layers of the aura. The subject may also be requested by the instructor to mentally expand their energy field for the observation of those present.

Various members of the group may be selected to participant as subjects for auric viewing. Having a variety of different subjects increases psychic sensitivity by providing comparison between the different energies displayed.

EXERCISE 12

Reading the Aura

Subject sits in front of the group. Participants mentally attempt to tune into the aura and discern specific information relating to the physical, mental and spiritual life of the individual. The teacher leading the exercise may ask questions about the subject concerning the past and present conditions of the individual. At which spontaneously participants tune in and respond according to what they feel the answer would be. The subject should keep completely silent while this is taking place and not provide any verbal or physical response. Questions that could possibly be asked include:

General questions about the past such as, "What was the subjects childhood like?" or: "What was his or her favorite pet?" And more specific questions such as: "What was his or her favorite toy?" or: "What was the name of his or her favorite teacher?"

In regards to the present questions may be asked about general things in his or her life such as: "What types of movies does he or she like to watch?" or: "What is his or her favorite food?" As well as more specific questions such as: "How much money does he or she have in their purse or wallet?" or: "What is his or her phone number?"

Teachers should link with their own spirit teachers who in turn will mentally influence them and suggest questions to ask the participants to attempt to psychically discern. At the end of the exercise the subject may share feedback with the members of the group. A number of participants may serve as subjects for this exercise.

Psychometry Exercises

EXERCISE 13

Basic Object Reading

The teacher requests students to place physical object for psychometry to be placed in a container. The students should pick an object that no one knows anything about. Keys or pieces of jewelry carried or worn on the person all the time are ideal as they hold much energy that has been absorbed from the owner.

The teacher stands holding the container behind themselves out of the view of those present. Individually each participant places their selected object into the container without saying anything least the teacher match the sound of their voice with the sound of the object.

Once all circle members, including the circle leader or teacher, have placed his and her objects in the container a guided meditation may follow, after which participants may each select an object to use for psychometry.

The teacher should explain the difference between psychic and mediumistic links. Since spontaneity is important for any psychic work, little time should elapse between the participants selecting an object, tuning in and sharing what they have received. Each participant should show his or her selected object, so that the owner will know that their object has been chosen and will pay attention. Only the participant should speak with feedback offered only after everyone in the group has taken their turn in sharing.

When tuning in the teacher may request that participants work either first psychically and providing details and descriptions of the owner of the object and then linking in mediumistically and bringing through spirit communicators and guidance for the recipient. While a participant is working with an object it is important that the owner of the item remain silent and not share. At the end of the exercise participants can give each other feedback.

Psychometry as an practical exercise is excellent as it helps the student of mediumship, not knowing anything about the owner of the object, keep their own logical mind out of the way. The less that the medium knows about the object the better.

There are variations of how psychometry may be practiced as a group exercise. In the past, many mediums used what is known as a ***psychometry box***, a wooden, rectangular box constructed with individual smaller sections, in which items could individually be placed to prevent the mixing of vibrations from taking place.

EXERCISE 14

Unknown Object in Box

The teacher places a box containing an object unknown to the participants in the group. The teacher, of course, should know the complete history of the object and those connected with it. After a period of meditation participants mentally tune into the contents of the box from a distance and report what they receive. The teacher may also request them to link in to the spirit world and bring through spirit communicators with messages.

After attempts have been made to tune in without physical contact, the box may be passed around with each participant spending a moment to tune in and try to psychically discern the nature of the contents as well as connect mediumistically. At the conclusion of the exercise feedback may be given by the teacher.

EXERCISE 15

Billets

The teacher hands out small slips of folded paper in which each participants writes a question. The folded papers may be either numbered beforehand or marked by the participant for identification. The same procedures as in exercise 13 may be followed with participants taking turns by selecting a billet and bringing through spirit communications. Prior to sharing participants should make sure to tell the others that the number or identification marks of the billet that they are working with. Other participants should be careful not to say anything or provide feedback while the billets are being read. At the end of the exercise feedback may be given.

EXERCISE 16

Questions in Sealed Envelope

Each participant writes a question on paper and places it in a sealed envelope. The same procedures may be followed as in exercise 13 with each participant linking directly to the spirit world and bringing through spirit communicators and messages. Ideally the question will be answered. Feedback may be given at the end of the session.

EXERCISE 17

Colored Ribbons

The same procedures as exercise 13 may be applied with colored ribbons being selected by participant who may work psychically and proceed to a mediumistic link. Feedback may be given at the end of the session.

EXERCISE 18

Candles

Each participant places a candle on a table. After meditation candles are lit and each participant selects a candle and links into the spirit world with a spirit message for the owner of the candle. This is an especially beautiful exercise to do in the evening around the Christmas holiday season.

EXERCISE 19

Flower Psychometry

Participants bring flowers or sections of plants that are placed on a table. Following the same procedures as exercise 13, after mediation participants take turns selecting and reading a flower. The flower may be initially read psychically with the stalk representing the past, the stem the present and the petals the future or by making a direct link to the spirit world. Flowers absorb the vibrations of the recipient and as such are excellent tools for this sort of experimental exercise.

EXERCISE 20

Speed Psychometry or Billets

Note, this is an extremely effective exercise in helping students of mediumship develop quick and spontaneous articulation of the impressions that they receive psychically and mediumistically. This exercise may be done with using physical objects, questions in sealed envelopes or billets placed in a container.

Teacher selects individual participants to stand in front of group and quickly pick items from basket and share what they are receiving. The teacher may time the participant giving them one minute with each item before cutting them off.

EXERCISE 21

Chair Psychometry

One member of group leaves the room. While this participant is absent, the teacher selects the chair of another member of the group and places it in the center of the circle. Upon returning the student medium sits in the chair and attempts to link either psychically with the energy of the person associated with the chair or mediumistically with the spirit world.

EXERCISE 22

Blindfold Psychometry or Billets

Exercises 13-23 all may be done with the medium blindfolded as well as under a deeper level of spirit control. While the use of blindfolds in mediumship is often done for the showbiz affect, as a tool they function to keep light out of the eyes of the medium and as such induce clairvoyant and trance states. The famous American medium Arthur Ford would always blindfold himself prior to bringing through Fletcher, his spirit control. T. Jack Kelly, the dynamic Lily Dale medium, would similarly work blindfolded and entranced while demonstrating clairvoyance from the platform. It is for this reason that blindfolds composed of thicker material are recommended.

EXERCISE 23

Photo Reading

A photo or photos unknown to the participants is presented. Participants are led into the meditative state by the teacher, After which each takes turns psychically tuning into the photo and attempting provide information about the person in the photo. Participants may also work mediumistically. It is important for feedback purposes that either the teacher or someone else knows the details of the individuals in the photos. This exercise may also be done by placing the photo in a sealed envelope.

1. National Spiritualist Association of Churches, *NSAC Spiritualist Manual* (14th Edition), Cassadaga, Florida,1987. p.40.

2. Ibid.

CHAPTER 2

The Development Circle

When the religious movement of Modern Spiritualism swept the planet in the mid-19th-century, the mediums experiencing communication from the spirit world had no formal training in the process of mediumship. Through trial and error and intuitive guidance from their mentors in the spirit world, the mediums of this period learned how to perfect their abilities, and better serve the spirit world as instruments for the higher teachings, guidance and healing needing to be imparted. The spirit personalities over time instructed students of spirit communication in scientific methods that when adhered to resulted in proper development of the mediumistic faculties. The higher spirit teachers in charge of training mediums encouraged groups of people to join together to sit for the purpose of developing stronger and better connections with the spirit world.

During the early years of the Spiritualist movement it was common for family and friends to meet regularly in the comfortable atmosphere of the home and sit for mediumship development. It was found that the positioning of participants in a circle affected the results of the spirit communications or phenomena experienced. When participants sat in the proper positions the psychic vibrations generated sufficient power for the spirit personalities to use for communicating and producing various phenomena. These type of closely knit, harmonious groups became known as *home circles* and in the early years of Spiritualism were the backbone of the rapidly spreading worldwide movement.

Regular attendance and participation in a development circle is essential for any serious student of mediumship. It does not matter a medium's level of experience as the process of mediumistic development is never-ending. Attunement with the spirit world may always be improved upon and enhanced. For this reason it is crucial for students of mediumship to sit in a properly run circle at least once a week.

Pauline's Open Circle

When it comes to development circles there are as many ways to run them as there are teachers of mediumship. In my study of mediumship, I have participated in many circles led by various teachers and with a variety of focuses. The first regular circle that I sat in was facilitated by the late Pauline Hathaway at the Church of Two Worlds in Washington, DC.

Pauline's group was an open circle in that anyone could attend with no obligation to participant in every session. In the years that I attended Pauline's circle, I found each session was a unique experience with regulars as well as new people coming and going, and the energy at each circle shifting in response to those in attendance at the particular session. Pauline's circle was pretty basic and served as an introduction to the science, philosophy and religion of Spiritualism and spirit communication.

The first part of the class would be a discussion on a topic related to Spiritualism, or a practical experimental exercise such as psychometry, which would be followed by a psychic circle involving meditation and the giving of spirit messages. Each class would always begin with a prayer followed by the members of the group choosing an affirmation from a sheet to be chanted in unison to raise the vibrations and make the atmosphere of the room conducive for spirit communication. This would be followed by a short guided meditation involving the sending of absent healing to people at a distance, during which participants would say aloud or quietly to themselves the names of loved ones or others in need of mental or physical healing.

After this period of healing, Pauline would continue the meditation for a short length of time and then open the circle up for giving psychic impressions or spirit messages for others present or the group as a whole. Depending upon the evening this part of the circle could be quite lively with participants spontaneously tuning in and conveying the spirit messages received for others in the group. The circle would end with a prayer by Pauline and by going around the circle with everyone expressing gratitude to God and their individual guides for the session.

Sylvia's Home Circle

At the very first Saturday afternoon circle of Pauline's that I attended, I met Sylvia and Joseph Giunta (both deceased), who had moved to the Washington, DC area from upstate New York. A student of mediumship for many years, Sylvia had developed her abilities in a home circle conducted by a prominent medium at the Lily Dale Assembly, a Spiritualist community in western New York. A medical doctor, Joseph's introduction to Spiritualism and psychic development took place after meeting and marrying Sylvia. Sylvia had facilitated circles for many years and invited me and several others in Pauline's class to attend a home circle that she was forming at her residence.

Sylvia ran her home circles in a completely different manner from the way Pauline conducted them. Although Sylvia's circles were by invitation only, it was not mandatory that participants attend each week.

Unlike Pauline, there was no formal class with a discussion or experimental exercises. Instead, after an initial prayer to start the proceedings, a guided meditation would be given to relax and heal the body and mind. This would be followed by a journey meditation to raise and harmonize the collective energy as well as help participants achieve the proper mental receptivity.

After the guided meditation we would sit in the silence for at least 45 minutes or more. Sylvia would also during this period allow various spirit teachers to entrance her and deliver philosophical discourses. Eventually, after sitting in quiet meditation, we would return to regular consciousness and share experiences and spirit messages with the group. At end of the circle, we would send absent healing to people at a distance and say a closing prayer. Unlike Pauline, who led all the prayers and meditations herself, Sylvia would choose different people to conduct prayers and guided meditations.

During my early training as a medium I attended as many development circles as possible. While Pauline's and Sylvia's circles were competently facilitated, other circles that I attended lacked structure and were poorly run by individuals who did not know what they were doing.

Benefits of Sitting

How does a circle help with mediumship development? It provides an educational environment where student mediums can learn to go into a receptive state and properly receive and convey spirit messages or produce mediumistic phenomena. The raised vibrations and collective energy of the group create a group energy field through which the spirit personalities are able to lower their rate of vibration in order to blend with the energy of the circle participants.

A good circle is not only about training the physical mediums, but it also includes training the spirit personalities to work with their individual mediums. The development of mediumship involves subtle adjustments made by helpers that affect the physical and energetic chemistry of the medium. These chemical changes gradually take place while the medium is sitting in meditation and not when they are giving out messages or channeling. The team of spirit personalities involved in training the medium will directly work with the chemistry of the developing medium during the circle while they are sitting in a meditative state.

Fundamental Points

A development circle needs to meet regularly, ideally at least once a week, at the same time and location. Five to eight participants is a good number for a circle, although any size will potentially work. What matters most is the enthusiasm and love that is present. The more positive energy present the more harmonious the psychic atmosphere will be. With larger numbers it is harder to achieve the energetic cohesiveness found within smaller groups. Of course, sometimes a smaller group will suffer due to insufficient power being available.

Punctuality and attendance at all meetings is important for circle participants. While some groups meet as open circles, for the best results closed circles are generally superior as the energy is consistent and built upon week after week by the spirit operators. Open groups are ideal in that an opportunity is provided for new people to check out mediumship development as well as people who, for whatever reason, are unable to commit to attending a weekly closed group.

The seating arrangement of the group is important. An ideal circle is composed equally of both genders, in which case the seating should alternate between male and female participants. Because the polarity is different between the genders this seating arrangement creates a strong battery of power that the spirit personalities are able to use to bring through communications, produce manifestations and develop the participants individually and collectively.

It is a fact that some people are stronger batteries than others. Positioning certain individuals in particular locations within the circle will greatly enhance the proceedings. It is also true seating certain people next to others and in a particular arrangement creates harmonious conditions. Each circle should be facilitated by an experienced medium or someone possessing knowledge about the mechanics of mediumship and the proper procedure for running a development group. Such a circle leader learns to rely on his or her intuition when leading the group in order to create the optimum, harmonious conditions conducive for the development of quality mediumship.

The spirit teachers working through the circle leader generally direct the seating arrangements necessary for the best possible results. Once the seating of the circle is determined for the participants, unless advised to do otherwise by the spirit teachers, it is essential that such arrangements are strictly adhered to.

Location

It is also important to choose the room or space used for the circle carefully. The best possible space for mediumship development circles is well-ventilated, and climate-controlled. It is important that temperatures are able to be adjusted depending upon the season. If the room is too hot or cold, or stuffy, then the circle members will experience discomfort affecting the results.

The space should be located where outside noise such as loud traffic or distractions will not affect the proceedings. While the circle is taking place turn off phone lines and cell phones. Dim the lights and consider light control options. Lighting may be dim, pitch black or illuminated by a red or blue bulb depending upon what is needed and the type of mediumship being developed. A lit cigarette is easily noticed in a darkened room, similarly subdued or no lighting helps participants notice the psychic impressions they receive. Red or blue lighting is best utilized for the development of physical mediumship as it allows participants to observe the proceedings without affecting the production of ectoplasm, a substance that reacts strongly to white light.

Seating

Proper seating is essential for circle work. I always prefer natural material when it comes to furniture and wood is great as a conductor for psychic energy. Make sure the chairs are comfortable and, if necessary, use cushions for back support. There is nothing worse than being unable to relax due to physical discomfort caused by sitting in chair with improper back support.

Chairs that are too soft and induce sleep are not good either as circle participants need to be mentally alert. For trance work, chairs with arms work well by providing support for the hands and arms of the medium. In many circles, the same chairs are kept in the room at all times in the same position and used only by the circle members for the mediumship work. Ideally, the room used for circle work should only be used for meditation, circle work, mediumship sessions, and spiritual healing.

Generally, it is best to arrange the chairs in a circle, although for some circles specializing in certain phases of physical mediumship or trance speaking, the chairs are arranged in a the shape of a horseshoe with the circle leader or medium being energetically focused upon in the open section.

Sitters

Participants should arrive on time and eager to commune with the spirit world with reverence and respect for the proceedings. Alcohol and other intoxicants, consumed even in small amounts on the day of the meeting, must be completely avoided as they pollute the vibrations and create disharmonious conditions. In the past, many of the Spiritualists attending home circles would bathe beforehand and wear fresh, clean clothes. While this may be impractical depending upon the situation, as a principle it encourages an attitude of reverence within. Cleaning the body and wearing fresh clothes externally brings cleanliness into the circle both physically and subtly as the clothes worn in daily life absorb denser material energies.

It is good to eat a light meal an hour and a half or two before the session. Too much food weighs down the physical body with an active digestive system and makes it difficult for the participant to achieve a deeper altered-state. Great amounts of psychic force are used for the circle and the energy is generated from the solar plexus center. An active digestive system makes this harder to accomplish and potentially gets in the way of proper attunement. Of course, most people would be uncomfortable on a completely empty stomach, which is why it is important to eat a light meal beforehand.

Participants should attempt to arrive at the circle around 15 minutes before the scheduled session is to begin. Arriving harried or stressed due to the anxiety of trying to get there on time should be avoided. An early arrival allows adequate time to relax and settle into the right state of mind. Anxiety or mental tenseness does the exact opposite. Problems of a personal nature also need to be left outside the door, although, realistically, this may not always be humanly possible. Keeping this point in mind, it is beneficial for creating the right mental state for the leader to conduct a short healing meditation to relax the physical body and rid the mind of unnecessary anxieties and problems.

A Few Essential Rules for Sitters

Be on time for the circle. If you are going to be late or cannot attend have the courtesy to call the circle leader to let them know your situation.

Once the circle starts, unless requested to do by the circle leader, do not get up or move about. Stay in your chair at all times as sudden movement may disrupt the delicate energies that have built up.

Obey the circle leader at all times. Trust his or her judgment and connection with the spirit world. If you do not feel comfortable with the circle leader, then you should not be attending circle with him or her.

Retain confidentiality at all times in terms of what has taken place in the circle with other participants. Do not do gossip or discuss intimate details of others in the circle outside of the group.

Be selfless and enthusiastic to learn.

Creating the Power

A circle should always be opened with a prayer invoking the Divine presence and asking that the highest and best of the spirit teachers and helpers assist with the proceedings. Sincere, heartfelt prayer helps create the proper reverence and spiritual atmosphere for the meeting.

Singing and music greatly assist the process of raising the vibrations and harmonizing the energy of the group. As far as I am concerned, when it comes to running circles, the more singing the better. A guitar or other musical instrument may be used to accompany the singing resulting in an even higher vibration. The songs or chants sung should be ones that participants know and enjoy. It has been found that faster and upbeat songs work the best for generating massive amounts of psychic energy that create an atmosphere suitable for the production of physical phenomena. Both slower and faster paced songs work well for raising the vibrations for mental mediumship.

Neither Pauline nor Sylvia had the members of their circles sing. Although Pauline did use the chanting of affirmations to raise the vibrations, which is also another way to actively build the power. For years I would have participants in my circles, after my opening prayer, recite *The Lord's Prayer* as I discovered that group chanting of prayers or affirmations along with loud and happy singing does much to create a powerful psychic atmosphere.

Feeling emotionally happy and light is important for creating the best conditions. While being serious and having reverence are also important, being too uptight and rigid destroys the conditions, as does anxiety, negative skepticism, competitiveness between participants, prejudice or issues with others in the group. Part of why home circles work so well is because of the harmonious conditions found between close friends and family united in their efforts to commune with loved ones and higher guides in the spirit world.

Procedure

After the opening prayer and singing, a short meditation to bring healing throughout the body may be given followed by a longer guided journey. The individual leading the guided meditation will find themselves often overshadowed or considerably influenced by the spirit teachers working with the group and be directed in terms of the meditation given.

Playing music greatly assists the guided meditation. Different types of meditative music achieve different results so it is important for the circle leader to select meditative music that they and the others in the group personally feel comfortable with and produces the desired result on the part of what needs to be accomplished. Music also helps block out distracting external noises and facilitates deeper levels of physical relaxation, mental receptivity and attunement to the spirit world.

Meditating completely in the silence and presence of the power without music is also extremely powerful. It really depends upon what needs to be accomplished and the nature of the group. A good circle leader is guided by the spirit teachers to work with the circle a particular way and make the appropriate adjustments as necessary. None of this is written in stone as what matters the most is doing what works with the circle to get the best possible results.

After the guided meditation the group may sit in the presence of the power for a period of time. Again, during this period, meditative music may or may not be used. The length of time participants sit in meditation varies. My preference is to keep my students in the meditative state for at least a half hour to an hour. This allows for the power to sufficiently build and the spirit operators to work with the chemistry of the participants and mentally connect with them. The length of time can be adjusted for inexperienced sitters.

Some circles spend little time in meditation and instead participants are encouraged to spontaneously give spirit messages as they receive them for others in the group. This was the approach that my teacher Pauline used in her class and other instructors I have known have used as well. The positive aspect of this approach is that students of mediumship actively learn how to work with the energy and give out spirit communications as they receive them. Spontaneous linking with the spirit world is an important skill for developing mediums to acquire. The drawback to this approach is that the actual development of mediumship does not take place during the delivery of spirit messages, but occurs in the period of meditation when the energy is built up. It is when the participants calmly sit in the presence of the circle's power that the spirit team works with their chemistry and strengthens the energetic and telepathic connections.

At the end of the meditative period participants are gradually brought back to regular consciousness. The circle leader needs to make sure that everyone has come back, which is accomplished by proceeding clockwise around the circle and having people affirm that they are back.

Next, participants may take turns sharing what they have experienced and, if received, giving spirit messages to others or the group as a whole. During this period it is important that the circle leader encourage everyone to participate and share. Generally, for reasons of etiquette and order, only one person should speak at once.

After all participates have shared, the session may be concluded with everyone standing and holding hands. A healing prayer may be recited collectively along with affirmations for the healing of self and those at a distance. A closing prayer should be given at end of the circle expressing gratitude to God and the spirit personalities for the healing and inspiration experienced during the meeting. Students should also discipline themselves to psychically close down at the end of the meeting.

Voice Vibration

I insist that students in my development circles get in the habit, from day one, to ask recipients for permission to come to them with a spirit message. I do this so that students learn proper etiquette. We should never assume that someone attending a mediumship demonstration wants to receive a spirit message. There could be many reasons why they do not want to receive it. Additionally, hearing the response of the recipient teaches student mediums to use the voice vibration to strengthen the connection. Mediumship is a two-way street with the medium being the go between. If we were talking on the phone with someone and the party on the other end did not respond, eventually we would conclude that they were not there and would hang up on them. Mediumship works the same way in that sound vibration assists and strengthens the connection between the physical and spiritual worlds. This is also why singing and music are essential for circle and seance work.

I remember once in Calgary, Canada doing a Sunday evening Spiritualist worship service. The first person that I was drawn to was a gentleman sitting in the back. "May I come to you?" I asked. "No!" was the reply. I will not speculate on the reasons why he did not wish to receive a spirit message, I have experienced people refuse to receive a spirit messages on a number of occasions and, in each case, I honor their wishes and continue delivering communications to other recipients.

Spiritual Healing Enhances the Power

I like to include hands on spiritual healing with the development circles that I conduct. Usually I will have hands-on healing take place after the meditation and sharing with participates pairing up and taking turns channeling healing for each other. Generally, by this point the power present is incredible, which is why in the circles that I run absent healing is also given at the very end. Hands-on spiritual healing may also be alternately given prior to the meditation and circle by participants pairing up and exchanging healing. While the power generally is not as strong as it would be after the meditation, sharing healing before helps build the power and creates a greater cohesiveness between circle participants, which will help the results of the circle.

Types of Circles

There are many different approaches to running a development circle and formats widely vary between circle leaders. The format or structure also depends on the experience of the participants and the focus in terms of mediumistic development.

Open Circle

The open circle provides an opportunity for new people to check the proceedings out as well as giving those unable to attend regularly a chance to sit. Due to the fact that new participants are regularly coming to the group, it enables students of mediumship the chance to practice bringing through spirit messages for different people each week. This is something that cannot be done with a closed circle, in which the people are always the same. The energy in open circles tends to change from week to week and lacks the consistency generally found in closed circles. Many Spiritualist centers offer open circles, which provide a good introduction to the study of mediumship.

Closed Circle

The closed circle is open only to those selected to participate and as such the energy builds with each session growing stronger and more cohesive over time. A closed circle maybe run for participants at any level of experience. In some cases, such a circle may be held regularly for years with the same participants attending week after week. Closed circles may also be run for a set period of weeks or months.

In a closed circle, it is mandatory that participants attend each week. It is suggested that circle leaders interview potential participants prior to beginning the circle for the purpose of determining their level of experience, commitment, and potential issues, personal or professional, which might affect their ability to attend regularly. Since harmony is essential for success in any group, the circle leader needs to assess the potential participant energetically in terms of their compatibility with other participants. A sincere individual will still adversely affect the results of a circle if his or her chemistry is not harmonious with the others in the group.

Obviously, there may always be emergencies or situations that come up beyond the participants control. However, it is extremely important that once the commitment to attend is made that it is kept. Many development circle leaders allow only one or two absences from circle members regardless of the reason. Any more results in the dismissal of the participant from the group. Consistent attendance is essential as the absence of one member from a closed circle changes the entire chemistry of the group and may potentially affect the results in a disastrous way. In any case, circle leaders must trust their intuition in such situations and respond accordingly.

Closed groups may be held in a private residence or a Spiritualist church or center. A closed circle may be geared toward a particular level of experience in terms of the participants or a specific phase of mediumship such as trance, transfiguration, or spiritual healing.

Mental Mediumship Circle

In this type of circle emphasis is placed on the development of clairvoyance, clairsentience and clairaudience and utilizing these mediumship phases for private sessions and larger public demonstrations.

Sample Format for Mental Mediumship Circle

- Opening prayer
- Singing for raising the vibrations
- Guided meditation for healing and relaxing the body
- Guided journey meditation to connect with spirit teachers and helpers
- Period of sitting in meditation with or without music
- Sharing of experiences and delivery of any spirit messages received.
- Hands-on spiritual healing
- Healing prayers and absent healing
- Closing prayer

Trance Circle

A trance circle focuses on the development of trance speaking for one or more of the participants. Chairs may be placed in a circle for the seating arrangement or a horseshoe format with the medium sitting for trance in the open section. Participants developing trance should take turns allowing spirit communicators to speak through them. When developing trance speaking, record sessions or have a circle scribe take detailed notes. The circle scribe should possess the skill of writing in shorthand and the ability to write in the dark or subdued lighting.

Healing Circle

A healing circle may be open or closed format with a focus on absent, self-healing, or hands-on spiritual healing. In addition to the standard opening and closing prayers, consider chanting positive affirmations and singing songs. Guided healing meditations, for self and absent healing, may be included along with hands-on spiritual healing. Instruction may be offered in all aspects of healing, including trance healing, psychic diagnosis and other specific techniques.

Psychic Awareness Circle

A basic psychic awareness circle is not focused on the development of mediumship, but instead concentrates on cultivating intuitive awareness, meditative skills and healing. A circle of this sort provides a comprehensive foundation for future mediumistic unfoldment. Basic meditation techniques may be practiced along with experimental exercises designed to enhance awareness of psychic abilities. A lecture and discussion period with this type of circle is also beneficial as it gives novices the time to ask questions and receive answers about basic concepts involving psychic development as a whole.

Physical Circles

The physical mediumship circle focuses on the development of physical phenomena. As such it is important that the circle be closed and the participants carefully screened and chosen. The format of a physical circle is dependent upon the phase of physical mediumship desired. Generally, seance work is done in a completely blackened room with absolutely no white light permitted due to the danger of harming the medium and inhibiting the production of ectoplasm.

Spirit Cabinets

A spirit cabinet may also be utilized to concentrate the energies for physical mediumship. Cabinets provide a dark, enclosed space for the medium to sit for the production of the phenomena. A cabinet may consist of simply a curtain draped across a corner or section of the seance room or a specially constructed curtained box. In all cases, the cabinet should allow for some room at the top of the curtained entrance and may even be placed upon a platform. A sturdy, yet comfortable seat for the medium is placed within the cabinet. The chairs may be placed in a horseshoe position or in some cases rows facing the cabinet. Cabinets are excellent for the development of materialization, etherialization, transfiguration and other physical phases of mediumship.

Spirit trumpets, musical instruments and other physical objects that can be used for the physical phenomena may be placed on a table, off to the sides of the cabinet or other locations around the room. It helps if the room is smaller with low ceilings as the energy is better contained in such premises. The lifeforce of fresh flowers and plants provide power and enhance the atmosphere.

Spirit Trumpets

Voice mediumship directly involving the trumpet, a type of psychic megaphone usually constructed out of aluminum, or independent without the trumpet, does not always require a cabinet, although the late Leslie Flint, a highly acclaimed British independent voice medium, had his own special cabinet made with a microphone placed overhead for amplifying the spirit voices.

The area around trumpets placed on the floor may be marked to determine the extent of any movement caused by the spirit personalities during the session should it take place. Another approach is to place the trumpet on a table or even on its side hanging from the ceiling. Luminous bands may be wrapped around the trumpet in order that its movement may be observed by all participants.

Slates and Other Devices

Slates for independent writing may be used in physical circles as well as artist materials for independent drawing or painting. Musical instruments and other devices may be placed in the seance room which the spirit personalities may use for phenomena. There is not just one type of physical mediumship, but many phases each of which requires a particular approach. The circle leader needs to carefully follow instructions from the spirit teachers in regards to all aspects of the procedure as the focus for each physical circle varies.

Table Tipping

Physical circles for table tipping require the participants comfortably seated around a table. In some cases participants take turns at the table while others present act as energetic batteries for the phenomena.

Transfiguration

For transfiguration mediumship, the lights with a dimmer for adjustments need to be positioned in such a way that the face of the medium is clearly visible. This way all present will be able to observe the transfigurations as they take place.

Outdoor Seances

Physical seances may also be held outdoors as the energy present in natural surroundings adds enormously to the power present. The pioneering Spiritualists involved with the early Spiritualist camp, the Onset Bay Spiritualist Association established in 1877 at Cape Cod, Massachusetts, held seances on boats as well as on Wicker Island in the bay. At the Wigwam Spiritualist Camp in Onset, there are slates on display from some of those seances, with writing and drawings independently produced by the spirit communicators. The famous physical mediums and brothers, Horatio and William Eddy of Chittenden, Vermont, held outdoor materialization seances in the moonlight, in which dozens of fully materialized spirit people of all shapes and sizes wearing elaborate costumes would allegedly appear for all to see.

CHAPTER 3

Helpers and Guides

All mediumship is a cooperative effort involving the medium and trained specialists in the spirit world. It is essential for developing mediums to understand the role of such personalities in the mechanics of spirit communication. We all have spirit guides, loved ones and others in the spirit world, who attempt to influence us by imparting loving, constructive guidance to assist with our spiritual and material lives. Even staunch atheists, hardened criminals and the psychologically imbalanced have spiritual guardians around them from the spirit world. Assistance from guides is not dependent upon belief, but it is objective reality. Whether or not someone is receptive to the influence of the spirit world is another matter, but the spirit personalities are there and through regular meditation their presence may more easily be discerned.

Guardians

Many religious traditions teach the concept of guardian angels who watch over people in the physical world and protect them from harm. There is much truth to this as every soul incarnated into a human body has individuals in the spirit world looking out for his or her spiritual welfare. Such guardians are generally not anyone related to the person, but instead are attracted spiritually and volunteer to assist the incarnate person throughout his or her life in the physical.

Guardian angels are connected with the soul before conception, when the consciousness enters the womb of the mother, until after the physical destruction of the body when he or she enters once again into the spirit world. The personalities who serve as our guardian angels, undoubtedly, have known us from our time between physical births in the spirit world, if not from shared experiences in prior physical incarnations.

Guides

Spirit guides are different from guardians, although some of them may work with us long-term for all or most of our physical lives. Spirit guides are drawn to us through the Law of Attraction. The spiritual and mental attributes contained within our personal energy fields attract spirit personalities on the same wavelength to work with us. In some cases, they may only be around a short period to assist with some specific project or concern that is affecting us.

There is always room for improvement within each of us and even an individual, whose heart is encased in negativity, is capable of reformation. Consider the dealings of an extremely sleazy and unethical politician, motivated by greed and personal ambition. Even the most unprincipled, corrupt person in government will have spiritual guardians present, who may have also been involved in politics or government. These benevolent spirit personalities will attempt to impart a positive influence encouraging ethical behavior and using the leadership position for the welfare of others.

Helpers

When it comes to the process of mediumship, I prefer to use the term *helper,* rather than guide. The carefully planned and orchestrated act of spirit messages received and delivered by a trained medium involves the assistance of individuals in the spirit world who specialize with such inter-dimensional communication. Even many experienced mediums are unaware of how much effort and planning goes on behind the scenes to make mediumship work. We only see the results when a spirit message is clear to the recipient, who may weep with joy and acknowledgement of the communicating loved one.

The Spirit Band

The Spirit Band is the team of helpers who assist each medium. Each of these individuals is a specialist in the process of mediumship. According to information received from the spirit world there is an inner band and an outer band. The inner band regularly work with the medium on a long-term basis, whereas the outer band assisting the medium come and goes as needed. An experienced medium may have many dozens of such specialized helpers and others working through them.

Spirit helpers are individuals who as part of their spiritual service chose to work with mediums in the physical world. I have done mediumship sessions for many colleagues of mine, also practicing mediums, and brought through their spirit helpers who formerly were experienced mediums in the physical world. In some cases the deceased mediums, acting as spirit helpers, were well-known Spiritualist ministers or mediums, and knew or were even involved in mentoring the recipient. This makes perfect sense as someone experienced with the mechanics of mediumship in the physical world would naturally be attracted to continuing to work with mediumship once passed over

When a medium describes spirit communicators, and brings through information about them for identification as well as personal messages, the medium is assisted by helpers who act as third parties to relay the messages. The fact that an individual is deceased does not necessarily mean that they are an expert on the mechanics of the process.

Individuals in the spirit world have to want to come through. No medium can call up any particular spirit personality regardless of how much money they are given for the service. The spirit world is all around us and the spirit people are generally eager to communicate with people in the physical world. However, the people in the spirit world cannot be forced to communicate and there are many reasons why they are not able to come through a medium even in the cases of when they want to communicate with us. Most spirits lack the skill and expertise to effectively communicate with their loved ones in the physical world. In some situations the spirit personality may need time for emotional healing, he or she may have other issues or things that he or she needs to work on, or he or she simply for other reasons may not be ready to come through.

Spirit loved ones have described to me how much time they had to spend with the helpers rehearsing the process and learning how to communicate. I have been aware of spirits, not related to myself observing mediumship sessions in order to learn the proscess to communicate through other mediums with loved ones in the physical world. Obviously, there are some personalities who make better communicators than others. An individual who is loud and extroverted may find it easier coming through than someone who is shy and introverted. And the more a spirit personality rehearses and practices the better he or she will be at communicating.

How long does it take for spirit people to come through once they pass over and go into the spirit world? I have had spirit people come through the very same day that they passed over. Once I was doing platform mediumship at a Spiritualist church and felt drawn with a message to a couple sitting in the back pews. I proceeded to bring through five spirit loved ones, who gave the recipient advice about some current situations that he was dealing with in his life. The man understood completely the guidance and recognized four of the five communicators. The following week the man approached me and explained that upon getting home the week before, his wife had received a phone call informing her of the death earlier that morning of a relative living in another state. This relative was recognized by the couple as the unidentified spirit in the message I had given them.

Another time I was serving another Spiritualist church in the Boston, Massachusetts area and brought through the father of a woman who attended the church. She could easily identify her father and understood the guidance that he conveyed through me. This woman was earnest and very active in psychic development and exploration. She attended sessions with prominent mediums regularly and even taught intuitive development and astrology classes in her home. She happily explained to me that this had been the first time her father had come through a medium ever and he had been in the spirit world at that point for 43 years. Why had it taken him so long to come through, especially considering the many sessions with numerous mediums that she had received over the years? There are many possible reasons why her father did not communicate, but the main point is to remember is that spirits cannot be called up and will come on their own accord.

Mediumship is telepathic communication and if a spirit loved ones finds a medium, who he or she mentally feels on the same wavelength with, the easier it will be for him or her to come through. A medium who is not in harmony with the spirit might be able to provide an accurate description and specific information about him or her such as his or her name, street address and telephone number, but the fullness of his or her personality would not necessarily be conveyed without a harmonious connection. When the communicating spirit is in mental harmony with the medium the results are superb and it will feel as though the spirit personality is right there speaking through the medium.

The members of the spirit team spend years studying with the medium. When the medium attends a development circle, they blend their thoughts with the medium's mind and energetically connect with the aura or energy field of the medium. Outside of the formal class situation they also spend time studying and learning about the nature of the medium. They especially attune with the medium during the medium's periods of private meditation and deep sleep.

The spirit helpers know everything about their medium. They are aware of the life history of the medium and his or her personal strengths and weaknesses. All the life experiences and formal education of the medium are stored deep within the unconscious mind. This includes the contents of every book that the medium has ever read, and every film or television show he or she has watched. It is such information that the spirit helpers access when it comes to transmitting mental messages through the medium to people in the physical world.

Master Teachers

Master teachers are part of the outer band of the medium. Generally, a master teacher was highly evolved spiritually when they lived in the physical world. The personal character and devotion to God of a master teacher motivates them to want to reach as many people as possible and awaken them to higher consciousness. Jesus, Lao Tzu, Confucius and Saint Francis of Assisi are all examples of master teachers. They impart wisdom and higher teachings to many and are concerned with enlightening humanity with God realization and spirituality. Such master teachers generally work through lesser spirit teachers who function as intermediaries with mediums in the physical world.

Doctor Teachers or Teachers of Philosophy

Teachers of philosophy possess great wisdom and may present themselves as a wise, elderly Chinese sage or a master from another cultural or religious tradition. They impart higher teachings through inspirational speaking and writing as well as deeper levels of controlled mediumship such as automatic writing or trance channeling.

Chemists

Part of the inner band spirit chemists work closely with the physical and subtle energies of the medium as well the energy of a smaller development group or seance or a larger mediumship demonstration. Chemists work with the spirit physicians to make sure the medium is in optimum health and that the mediumistic development of the medium is achieved to the highest potential.

Spirit Physicians

The spirit physician or healer may be a traditional Chinese energy worker or doctor, a Native American Indian medicine person or healer from another culture or tradition of healing. There are many modalities and approaches to healing. Mediums who work with spiritual healing attract many spirit healers to assist patients in the physical world. In the same way that there are physicians in the physical world who specialize in various aspects of medicine and alternative healthcare, the same is true in regards to spirit healers who operate through the medium as part of a larger healing team.

The spirit physicians pool their resources and based on the needs of the patient, the appropriate healers will diagnosis the patient and administer the necessary treatment. Spirit doctors along with the spirit chemists assist the medium with the process of development by imparting beneficial energies and helping the subtle and physical systems of the medium function efficiently in response to his or her mediumistic unfoldment. Spirit doctors are part of the inner band of the medium.

Doorkeepers

The doorkeeper or gatekeeper controls the situation in terms of who comes through the medium. Mediumship is a carefully planned process and it is the door keeper's responsibility to regulate the spirit personalities desiring to come through the medium. The door keeper is part of the inner band of the medium.

Runners

When the answers to questions asked by inquirers to the medium are not immediately known, the runner will attempt to quickly find the answer in the spirit world, so that the information is communicated through the medium to the inquirer in the physical world. According to some schools of Spiritualist thought, Native American Indians make excellent runners. The runner is part of the inner band of the medium.

Message Bearers

Message bearers act as intermediaries for messages from loved ones and others in the spirit world, who are unable to directly come through. Most mental mediumship involves the use of message bearers who provide evidential descriptions and details of spirit loved ones directly to the medium. Message bearers are part of the inner band of the medium.

Joy Guides

Joy guides manifest as small children bringing happiness and laughter to the seance proceedings. The gleeful energy that such personalities impart raise the psychic vibrations improving the overall conditions for communication. Often, joy guides have manifested as illiterate African-American children or other ethnic class. In many Spiritualist seances the use of the English language by such guides reinforced the worst possible stereotype of an uneducated child from whatever racial or ethnic background they allegedly were from.

A century ago it was not uncommon in honor of the Native American Indian guides for Spiritualists to dress up in Native American Indian garb and hold *Pow-Wows* for the purpose of communing with them.

Similarly many mainstream, Caucasian performers in the same era masqueraded as African-Americans by applying charcoal upon their faces.

Some instructors of mediumship teach that the main control or doorkeeper is always a small child or joy guide. The result of this concept is many mediums, allegedly controlled by such guides, will speak in squeaky voices and tell stupid jokes. This is not to say that a small child could not entrance a medium, but behavior lacking dignity and intelligence is generally due to the delusions or embellishments of the medium.

Native American Indians

It is common for Native American Indians as well as other indigenous people to work as helpers for mediumship. The various tribes of Native Americans were extremely psychic as a race and practiced mediumship and healing as part of their religious observances and culture. With the spread of the Spiritualist movement in the mid-19th-century many Native American Indians made themselves known as the guides for various mediums.

While the idea of Native American Indians as helpers may rightly sound absurd to many people, I know from my own experiences in teaching and demonstrating mediumship internationally that Native American Indians act as helpers for mediumship and healing for mediums living in many parts of the world. The denser vibrations of Native American Indians and similar indigenous people enable them to more readily be involved in the production of physical healing and seance phenomena. Spirit personalities operating at a higher frequency of vibration are also able to use them as intermediaries for communication through mediums.

There was a period in late 19th-century America that many within the Spiritualist movement considered Native American Indians to be less evolved as guides and as such not worthy of working with in that capacity. In response to this backward view a group of mediums in the Onset, Massachusetts Spiritualist community in 1893 organized the Onset Wigwam Spiritualist Camp for the purpose of spiritual healing and in honor of the Native American Indian healing guides. The Onset Wigwam continues to this day to hold Spiritualist meetings where members of the public can receive spiritual healing treatments and mediumistic communications.

There have been many prominent Native American Indian guides who have worked through mediums. The warrior Black Hawk, who fought the United States government, was famous as a guide for many mediums including the noted trumpet medium Hugh Gordon Burroughs, physical medium Jennie Lord and the pioneer of Spiritualism in New Orleans, Mother Leafy Anderson.

Healing Sisters

Healing Sisters are nuns or nurses dedicated to working with healing through the medium.

Protectors

The protector spirits serve closely with the medium and help regulate the process of communication. A trained medium with the assistance of such benevolent personalities in the spirit world is automatically provided protection from lower vibrations and ignorant, unauthorized spirit personalities.

Guide Worship

It is common for some mediums to name drop by stating that their spirit guides or teachers are famous personalities, perhaps biblical, historic or even deceased celebrities. Generally speaking this is complete delusion on the part of the medium or fraud. Many mediums seek to amaze and impress others with displays of their clairvoyant accuracy or important sounding names of famous or exotic guides.

I knew an extremely talented and charismatic British medium, who was entranced as a healer by an ancient Chinese doctor. It was amazing to see how many people, mainly female, worshiped the ground this medium walked on as well as the alleged spirit personality healing through him. As in many such cases the medium encouraged such worship and as an experienced medium gained a considerable following.

Unfortunately, the medium took advantage of some of his followers by engaging in inappropriate sexual relations with them. A number of his victims, all young women or teenagers, who had sought him out for healing, were severely damaged emotionally by their involvement with him and the violation of professional boundaries that took place.

The victims filed rape charges against the medium, which resulted in his arrest and criminal prosecution. According to the sworn testimonial of some of the young women the spirit doctor made statements such as: "In order to heal your cancer you need to go *all the way* with the medium." and: "You and the medium have a very special relationship. You were in the same Native American tribe in your past life."

This particular court case made front page news bringing the Spiritualist movement and mediumship in general in disrepute. Surprisingly, many Spiritualists believed that the accusers were either fabricating the allegations or that an evil entity entranced the medium to perform the alleged rapes and molestations. The medium was found guilty and sentenced to prison for his offenses. After a few years he was released for good behavior and continues to practice spiritual healing surrounded by his supporters and admirers.

Mediums should never be worshiped or placed on a pedestal. The same applies to spirit teachers and guides. The higher teachers and guides in the spirit world are always are always ethical and loving and will never order anyone to do anything. They do not pass judgment, but make constructive suggestions based on what is in the best and highest good for all concerned. Most importantly guides do not want to be put on a pedestal as all worship should go to God.

The higher spirit teachers encourage and empower people to think for themselves and make decisions that will be most beneficial for soul growth. They are not interested in titles, adoration or distinction, but care most about helping people in the physical world respond to the challenges of life in the most spiritual way possible. Although some people would like the spirit world to make decisions for them the spirit teachers will never make the choices for us as we are the captains of our own ships and must learn through our experiences that we must take responsibility for our spiritual progression.

Common Sense

It is always important for people to never throw out their common sense when receiving communications purportedly from the spirit world. Many years ago a client of mine in Hollywood contacted me as he wanted me to ascertain the authenticity of a series of manuscripts that he had channeled mediumistically. According to my client he had received the information clairaudiently writing it down verbatim. I looked over the thousand pages of philosophy allegedly given to him by numerous deceased historic figures and celebrities such as Abraham Lincoln, Albert Einstein and Janis Joplin. Some of the ideas expressed were interesting while other parts were completely bizarre, most notably sections dealing with my client's special spiritual mission and position as *the Second Coming of Christ.*

A number of the messages were purportedly conveyed by Jerry Garcia, the deceased lead singer for the hippy band, *the Grateful Dead* widely known for their lengthy jams and use of mind-altering substances. Upon questioning my client further about the specific circumstances he received the channeled information, he revealed that he had smoked large quantities of marijuana prior to his psychic sessions. I am not sure how much of the material he channeled was a product of his own drug induced delusions and how much could originated from personalities in the spirit world.

This is not to say that celebrities or well-known public figures are not able to communicate. I knew a Canadian medium at the Lily Dale Assembly in New York, who brought through Albert Einstein for a man in attendance at a large outdoor public meeting. The recipient of the communication knew Einstein as a neighbor causally in the 1940's and was able to identify him by the evidential description provided by the medium. I have had similar experiences with individuals coming through from the spirit world who had been famous when they were physically present. In every case, the information that came through was specific and evidential for the recipient, who was related to or knew the communicating spirit personally. Another medium I knew once did a session for Elvis Presley's manager in Las Vegas and stammered in the same manner as the deceased singer as she delivered the information coming through from him. The communication completely floored the manager as he had told her absolutely nothing about his background.

Mediumship is always about teamwork and trust. Developing mediums should always use their common sense and cultivate an intelligent, working relationship with their band of helpers. It is easy to get sidetracked with worshiping guides or believing that high-level masters are personally tipping the living room table. Spirit helpers are motivated by love and work through mediums for the purpose of assisting those in need. It is the responsibility of developing mediums to harmonious blend their minds and energies with their team of helpers.

CHAPTER 4

The ABC's of Clairvoyance

Clairvoyance is a French term that means *clear seeing*. It is a phase of mental mediumship, which many students of psychic development and mediumship seek to acquire: "I want to see dead people. I want to see what is going to happen in the future." There are several types of clairvoyance that may be experienced as a developing medium.

Objective Clairvoyance

Objective clairvoyance is a rare phase of mediumship and when it takes place it will seem to the medium that the spirit people viewed are as solid and real as physically bodied people. The medium will not even necessarily realize at first that what he or she is seeing is clairvoyant as it seems as though he or she is seeing the forms with his or her physical eyes. Although for this reason objective clairvoyant is termed as such, in reality it is a subjective experience which takes place through the direct vision of the subtle body acting through the physical eyes.

Subjective Clairvoyance

Subjective clairvoyance involves the medium's mind receiving mental impressions of images, literal and symbolic as well as visual depictions of spirit people. In order for subjective clairvoyance to take place the medium's mind must be properly attuned. Subjective clairvoyance is the most common form of clairvoyance and functions in conjunction with clairsentience and clairaudience.

X-ray Clairvoyance

X-ray clairvoyance is the form of psychic seeing in which solid matter is penetrated by the vision of the medium. Mediums experiencing such clairvoyance feel as though they are able to see through physical matter objectively with their physical eyes. X-ray clairvoyance is a rare phase of mediumship most effectively used for the diagnosing of health conditions and the reading the contents of sealed envelopes or packages.

Traveling Clairvoyance

Traveling clairvoyance or remote viewing is the psychic ability to view locations at a distance. Often confused with astral or out-of-body travel, traveling clairvoyance differs in that the subtle body does not project or leave the physical body as with astral travel. During the functioning of traveling clairvoyance the medium may be in varying degrees of altered-consciousness. There are deeper trance states in which traveling clairvoyance or even out-of-body travel may take place with the unconscious medium speaking about what he or she is seeing at a distance while in the trance state.

Trance Control Clairvoyance

Trance control clairvoyance involves the spirits controlling the medium describing what they are experiencing from their view in the spirit world. Subjective clairvoyance, in which the medium is generally in a lighter state-of-altered-consciousness, may easily lead to a deeper state of entrancement with the spirit personalities controlling the medium and directly speaking.

The Stages of Clairvoyant Unfoldment

The first step needed to develop clairvoyance is learning how to declutter and quiet the mind so that it is receptive to the impressions from the spirit world. But how does one shut down the mind with its seeming endless thoughts about the problems and concerns of mundane life? It is completely impossible to make the mind go blank as the nature of the mind is to be active.

The process of quieting the mind is achieved through learning how to progressively relax the physical body, both accomplished by mind focus and breathing exercises. A tense physical body leads to an unreceptive state of mind filled with tension and lacking focus. Breathing should be deep and rhythmic involving the lower abdomen and not just the upper chest.

Sitting comfortably with the spine erect, feet flat on the floor, legs and arms uncrossed with palms facing up to receive, is a proper position conducive for meditation and receiving spirit communication. Once the mind is receptive the student will perceive many flickering and random images that appear within the inner mirror of the mind. In the beginning such images will appear to be completely products of the student medium's own imagination originating from the unconscious mind. As more time is spent learning how to relax the body and still mental activity, the student medium gradually will notice increasingly more images appearing within his or her inner vision. Such images will flow together, one after another, almost in the same manner as a film.

The pictures seen within will not necessarily have any meaning. It is important at this stage that the student medium share what he or she is seeing with others in the development circle, even if he or she is uncertain the origins of such images or considers them products of his or her imagination. If such imagery is experienced by the student medium outside of a development circle during his or her personal meditations, then it should be carefully recorded in a note-book for future reference.

As discussed in Chapter 2 sharing such experiences with others in the circle is extremely important for several reasons. First, it lets others in the group know what the student medium has experienced, which helps others relate it to their own experiences during the meditation. Often people may see or sense similar things during a development circle, so sharing enables students to compare notes and experiences. Another important reason for sharing is that it helps the student medium get more in touch with his or her own inner vision. By expressing it aloud, student mediums become strongly aware of what they are experiencing in terms of imagery, feelings or other psychic sensations that may accompany it. Spirit helpers will be aware of what the student medium receives. If the student medium leaves some of it out, misinterprets the information, or embellishes it in any way, the spirit helpers will take note and adjust accordingly in terms of how they present it.

Many times, student mediums will sit in a development circle and not share what they are experiencing. Often, this is due to either inhibition, fear of being incorrect, or simply the dismissal of images due to thinking that they are meaningless products of the imagination. A student's error are part of the learning process. Sadly, many circle leaders do little or nothing to encourage sharing by the circle participants. Sharing helps students get in touch with their own inner vision and enables others to benefit from their experiences.

The constant flow of images is the beginning of true clairvoyance. Sometimes the flow may consist completely of faces of people unknown to the student medium. Such faces are those of the spirit people who are either working with the mediums development or wish to observe the proceedings for a variety of possible reasons. This is generally followed by the student medium being aware of one or two images that seem to stand out from other mental pictures. The student medium may push such images aside only to have them continue to reappear. Again, such images need to be expressed aloud when in a circle situation or recorded in a journal if experienced during private meditation. If one sits and says nothing the spirit helpers will not be certain that the image was properly received. In order to receive completely, one must empty his or her cup.

It is also typical at this stage for student mediums during meditation to see *pairs of eyes* within their inner mind. Such pairs of eyes often will resemble the eyes of animals looking out at you from the nighttime darkness of the thick forest. Images of eyes within the context of mediumship often symbolically represent spiritual vision as represented by the third eye at the forehead. Pairs of eyes also represent the idea of spirit personalities watching the student medium develop.

The seemingly endless stream of images seen within the inner mind of the student medium generally are completely meaningless by themselves. In fact, there usually is no symbolic meaning to them. Such images could be viewed as simply meaningless messages conveyed to see if they were received by the medium. At this stage the medium may feel drawn to others for the purpose of sharing the information. It is fairly common for student mediums sitting in a circle to energetically feel pulled or mentally directed to other participants sitting next or across from them.

The spirit helpers will begin to convey images that have symbolic meaning and that require interpretation on the part of the novice medium. The student medium may again feel drawn to others in the group with the message of what they are seeing. The message typically will be more generalized such as an image of a clown, which correctly interpreted means that the recipient needs to *joke around* more. A very generic message since it could apply to many in terms of advice.

The process of receiving clairvoyant messages may be compared to learning how to properly write. First, the alphabet must be learned, after which basic words such as cat and dog may be written followed by simple sentences such as, "See Spot run." or, "See Dick ride his bike." Once these elementary sentences are mastered a more sophisticated vocabulary may progressively be introduced using longer words in more complex sentences.

With clairvoyance the generic messages that could apply to just about anybody are gradually built upon by the spirit helpers who introduce images containing multi-levels of meaning both literal and symbolic. As a result the spirit messages conveyed by the medium increasingly become more specific in terms of content.

Seeing Spirits

Once the student medium feels comfortable receiving basic symbols, the spirit helpers will facilitate guides, loved ones and others in coming through. Mediums typically see the impressions of the spirit communicators within their own minds. In some cases the spirits may be imposed over the features of recipients or standing beside or behind them. The form of the spirit communicators may be extremely vivid in detail or transparent and vague.

Evidential Clairvoyant Observation

Mediums must learn to carefully observe the features and surroundings of the spirit communicators. The details within the visual information presented are crucial for providing irrefutable evidence of survival. The spirit team will structure the presentation of such information in a manner that is organized and clear. It is easy for mediums to overlook details within the clairvoyant images that might be extremely important. The formula or structure of the message is secondary to the development of good observation skills. The following checklist of information for clairvoyant observation is the same as found on suspect description forms used by law enforcement agencies for gathering information from witnesses.

Gender

- *Is the spirit communicator male, female or transgendered?*

Build

- *Is the spirit thin, medium, stocky or obese, etc?*

Height

- *Is the communicator tall, medium or petite, etc?*

Head Pieces

- *Is the spirit wearing anything on their head such hats or helmets, etc. If so, what is the style and era of the head piece? Is it military head-gear or worn by service personnel such as police officers, firefighters, etc.?*

Hair

- *What is the color and length of the hair of the spirit person? Are they bald and receding, etc? Is the hair style unkept, neatly combed, etc? What era is the hair style from? 1950's, 1970's, etc.*

Facial

- *What is the eye color of the spirit communicator? Are they wearing glasses or a molecule? And, if so, describe the era and style of the eyewear. Does the spirit personality have any facial hair such as a beard or mustache? Are there any scars or birth marks?*

Skin

- *Is the texture worn, youthful, wrinkled, etc?*
- *Are there any birth marks, scars. tattoos, etc?*

Age

- *Is the communicating spirit an infant, toddler, child, preteen, early-teen, mid-teen, late-teen, college age or an adult in his or her twenties, thirties, forties, fifties, etc?*

Clothes

- *Are the clothes of the spirit communicator neat, unkept or formal, etc?*
- *Is the clothing professional or causal?*
- *Any uniforms and, if military, what branch and what unit?*
- *Officer or enlisted? What era or what conflict?*

- *If the clothing is a service uniform? Police, fire fighter, janitor, nurse, nun, maid, etc?*
- *What era are clothes from? 1930's, 1960's, 1980's, etc?*

Footwear

- *Boots, causal shoes, barefoot, etc?*

Body Language

- *Standing erect, stooped over, weight on one leg, etc?*
- *Are there any body parts missing such as limbs or fingers, etc?*

Other Props

- *Wheel chair, walker, cane, crutches, etc?*

Objects Held

- *Flowers, tools, kitchen utensils, etc?*

Jewelry

- *Are they wearing rings, bracelets, crosses, prayer beads, etc?*

Location

- *Where do they seem to be?*
- *Rural or city? Outside or inside?*
- *Is it a residence, work place or other location?*
- *Is the location urban, suburban, or rural?*

Landmarks

- *Are there any landmarks nearby such as the ocean, lakes, railroad tracks, large cities, cemeteries, laundromats, etc?*

Buildings

- *What is the structure made of? What is the color, size and appearance?*
- *What is the address? Street and number?*

Interior

- *Is the inside tidy or messy?*
- *How is it furnished and decorated? Furniture, works of art, photographs, wall-paper, other items of significance, etc?*

Exercises for Clairvoyance

EXERCISE 24

Attention to Detail

Teacher covers a large tray with an assortment of different shaped, colored, and types of physical objects. Participants are shown the tray of objects for approximately one minute and must within that time frame note the details of the objects that they have observed on the tray. The tray is removed after the allotted time and participants are forced from memory to recollect and describe the details of the objects that were on the tray.

This exercise may be done repeatedly with the contents of the tray regularly changed. This purpose of this exercise is to strengthen participants awareness of small details. This will naturally result in an increase of clairvoyant awareness and ability to notice minute details that typically would go unnoticed.

EXERCISE 25

Evidential Reading with Clairvoyance

Participants pair up seated across from each other in two, evenly spaced straight lines. After a short meditation with emphasis on the third eye chakra at the forehead and attunement with the team of spirit helpers, the participants take the hands of their partners and proceed to bring through clairvoyant information. Emphasis is placed in this exercise on obtaining evidential information visually. After one side finishes the other side may work or in the case of musical chairs, one side may work with multiple partners, one after the other.

EXERCISE 26

The Psychic Cap

While meditating imagine at the area of the third eye that you are wearing a psychic band or cap. This band is tight and energetically feels warm around the head. During the process of clairvoyant development, it is typical for student mediums to experience this energetic sensation. By focusing awareness on the area of the third eye, this visualization helps to stimulate the development of clairvoyant ability.

EXERCISE 27

Elevator Button

During meditation imagine a large elevator button. See it clearly and distinctly. Now, polish that button and make it even more bright and shiny. Observe the button even more clearly, brighter and shinier than before. By focusing awareness on the third eye, this exercise stimulates the development of clairvoyant ability.

EXERCISE 28

Daily Visual Awareness

In daily life, pay close attention to the visual details around you. The colors, lines and shapes. Focus first on the general shape, size and color of an object and then concentrate on the finer details within the larger form. Pay attention visually to the details and feel as though you mentally are able to extend your awareness from your physical location to touch them with your mind. The more that a medium in daily life cultivates an awareness of physical form, color and line, the greater that such details will be noticed within the clairvoyant imagery received mediumistically.

EXERCISE 29

Encyclopedia of Symbology

For developing the clairvoyant ability to receive and interpret symbols study the symbology of various cultures, traditions, and religions. This information may be found online as well as within an encyclopedia of symbology. The spirit helpers use what is in the medium's mind and if an image has a particular meaning or interpretation to the medium they will present such information in that manner when conveying messages.

EXERCISE 30

Traveling Clairvoyance

A members of the group goes into another room and with supplied art material creates a shape or picture depicting an intense emotion or theme. The teacher leads the others in the group into a deep meditative state for the purpose of mentally projecting into the other room. Participants mentally travel to the target location and attempt to see the depiction and feel the overall emotion or idea represented. The members of the group using art material should depict the color, shape, and feeling of what they observed at a distance. After everyone has shared, feedback is given and the artwork produced in the experiment shown.

CHAPTER 5

Psychic Shorthand

Symbology for conveying clairvoyant images is a type of psychic shorthand utilized by the spirit helpers for the purpose of expediting communications. Symbols allow complex messages to be conveyed in a short amount of time as one picture is worth a thousand words. Based on life experience, personal preference and culture, images mean different things to different people. The image of a snake that represents good luck in Chinese culture may be interpreted as evil in another part of the world. In many European countries people wear black when mourning, whereas in some African regions white is worn at funerals.

When it comes to telepathic communication so much may be lost due to poor conditions, carelessness or misinterpretation on the part of the medium or misunderstanding on the part of the recipient. Efficiency in getting across to the medium what details need to be communicated accurately is what is most important in the process of mediumship. But the spirit world is so often limited by recipients, who ignorantly fail to provide the best conditions for mediumistic communication or want things done a certain way. Poorly trained mediums, who allow themselves to get in the way of receiving more or inaccurately convey what little information they are able to receive are also a major problem. Unfortunately, the messages needing to be mentally communicated by the spirit personalities cannot always be easily transmitted in a manner that mediums are able to receive, understand and accurately give out to the recipient.

Sometimes people ask questions regarding mediumship such as: "Why can't deceased loved ones just come through and give their names?" and: "Why are the messages that so many mediums give so vague?" Spirit people often do come through and provide their names and other details about themselves for the purpose of identification and providing evidence of survival. But when we examine the mechanics of the process we become aware of the factors that limit and restrict the process. Abstract ideas and feelings are easiest for the intuitive mind to to telepathically convey and receive.

As individual personalities we are far more than just a name. My name may be Stephen, but who am I really as a person? If I were to communicate through a medium what details about myself would indicate the essence of my identity as an individual? In Western culture the names John and Mary are easily mentally received. But it would be a challenge to receive ethnic names such as *Chiwetel Ejiofor* or *Adewale Akinnuoye-Agbaje.*

Even a highly developed clairaudient medium would potentially have problems receiving such names for the same reason that the possessor of such names in the physical world would undoubtedly have difficulty with other people being able to spell or pronounce them. An individual with such a name would likely be asked to repeat it several times and possibly spell it when giving it over the phone. Of course, in the native cultures, where such names originate, this would not be a problem in the same way.

In regards to the interpretation of symbols it is important to note that the spirit world uses material within the mind of the medium. The more information and life experience that the spirit helpers have to draw upon within the memory banks of the medium the better. As previous noted all the mediums life experience and education are stored on an unconscious level within the mind. This is why education is so important in relation to the development of mediumship. There are some mediums who will make statements such as: "I don't need to read books, my Ascended Masters teach me everything I need to know" or: "I am a natural medium, I don't need to sit in circle or go to classes." This sort of attitude is complete ignorance and only leads to inferior performance as a medium.

Consider the analogy of a piano that has not been properly maintained with many of its keys missing. If a genius concert pianist such as Chopin were to sit down and try to play a composition on such a piano what would the music sound like? The result would sound horrible due to the fact that the poor condition of the instrument would severely limit the brilliance of the master musician from being expressed. The same principle applies with spiritual mediumship. The more we learn and study, not just about mediumship or psychic development, but subjects that enrich and expand our intellect and spirituality, the more that we will attract higher spirits to work with us. The more knowledge and experience stored within our minds, the more material the spirit helpers involved with the process of mediumship will have to convey information. During the process of mediumship development, the spirit helpers familiarize themselves with the life and personality of the student medium and establish an intimate, telepathic rapport that allows them access to unconscious mind of the medium and all that it contains in terms of life history and education.

Student mediums should generally trust their own intuition and interpret the symbol based upon what it means to them and not upon interpretations given by others. However, I once suggested to participants attending one of my development classes to obtain an encyclopedia of symbols to help them understand how to interpret what they were receiving in terms of spirit communications. (See Exercise 29) One of my students, a lively fellow and class clown, who eventually obtained his certification as a medium and ordination as a Spiritualist minister, followed my guidance and purchased such a book that provided extensive examples of symbols and detailed interpretations. He spent several days reading and studying the book's content and ended up memorizing all the symbols and their interpretation and meaning according to the book. As a result his team of spirit helpers began to present the symbols that he had memorized with the interpretations that he had learned as detailed in the material that he had read.

Once in my early years of formal mediumship study, I had to fill in for the receptionist at the office where I was employed at that time in Washington, D.C. Since it was not very busy that day, I spent several hours making a list of all the symbols that my spirit helpers were using with me for communications. I had only been sitting in mediumship development circles for about two years at that point, but I discovered that I had about four hundred symbolic images used by my helpers to convey messages through me. I remember noticing at the time how the number of images utilized for my clairvoyance had increased.

In the beginning of development the symbols received tend to be basic, almost generic symbols that could apply to the majority of people. Over time, the amount of symbols used increases and the messages brought through for the recipients becomes increasingly sophisticated. The symbols used by the spirit world for communication through the medium in one sense are a sort of psychic vocabulary that expands along with the skill and experience of the medium.

"How does one interpret a symbol if one is not sure of the meaning?" This is an important question asked by many novice mediums. Clairvoyant images given by the spirit world for the purpose of interpretation by the medium in the vast majority of cases come with a feeling or idea as to the interpretation or meaning of the particular image. Student mediums when not sure about the interpretation of a particular symbolic image need to be aware of the feeling that accompanies the image they are receiving. They also need to trust their intuition asking themselves what the image means to them personally and verbalize what they are feeling in terms of the meaning to the recipient, not being concerned whether they are right or wrong or what the reaction of the recipient will be. Novice mediums may misinterpret what the symbol means by leaving parts of it out or adding their own embellishments.

It is Totally Fine to Make Mistakes

It is valuable for student mediums to make mistakes as this is how learning takes place and the spirit helpers will try to make adjustments accordingly. If a novice medium is not sure of the meaning of a particular message received, they need to pray and ask for assistance with the interpretation or meaning of the image. There is nothing wrong with asking more experienced mediums their opinion about possible interpretation of symbols, but ultimately student mediums should strive to pay close attention to the feeling that accompanies each image, rather than listen to the interpretations of others.

The Pea Pod Image

Most clairvoyant images received are accompanied by a feeling, but in some rare cases there is no feeling as to the meaning of the message. Once in Connecticut at a metaphysical retreat, I did a private session for a highly spiritual woman of Hungarian background. As I brought through what I was receiving from her loved ones and guides, she understood and could relate to all the information that I was giving her. As a teenager, this woman had been involved in the Hungarian uprising in 1956 against the Communist government, which was quickly suppressed by the violent intervention of the Soviet military.

One of the spirit communicators who I brought through for this woman was an elderly, grandmotherly woman, who I described in great detail and she dominated much of the session. The woman reacted favorably with recognition as I described the older woman and relayed practical guidance and evidential details. At one point the spirit woman showed me a *pod of green peas,* which try as I might, I could not intuitively feel any meaning or interpretation with the image being presented.

I did not want to misinterpret the message or try to make it mean something more than what it was. Part of me for this reason mentally hesitated as I considered whether I should even include it with the rest of the information that I was receiving. Fortunately, I listened to the feeling that came with the image that strongly emphasized that I needed to mention what I was seeing. When I included my vision of the pod of green peas with the details about the spirit woman, I had no idea how such a seemingly trivial and meaningless image could make sense to my client.

At the end of the session, my client explained that the grandmotherly woman had been a very dear, deeply spiritual friend, who had been like a mother or grandmother to her. She related to me how as a teenager in Budapest, she had been involved in the uprising against the Communist government and found herself being pursued in the city streets by Communist soldiers. As she tried to escape from being captured, she fled in panic down an alleyway only to find that it was a dead-end. As she frantically tried to find an outlet to the alley, she ran past an elderly woman sitting outside an open door shucking green peas. The elderly woman motioned to her to come inside her residence, thus saving her from being captured and potentially imprisoned by the Communist authorities. The grandmotherly spirit woman, whom I had brought through was this same woman, and from this point on, both my client and her had developed a very close, spiritual friendship and bond. It would have been easy to dismiss the image of the pod of green peas as being meaningless or a product of my imagination, but as this example demonstrates sometimes the most trivial or seemingly insignificant information may be the most evidential or meaningful for the recipient of the communication.

The Basics

In training mediums the spirit teachers will start by presenting basic symbols such as the image of a beach ball, which is typically associated by many people with the concepts of beaches, recreation and fun. Any medium could stand up in a packed auditorium and boldly tell several rows of people: "You need to play more and have more fun." Other than people with an occupation as a clown or children's entertainer, this is a totally generic message that could apply to practically everyone as the majority of people need to play more and would benefit by having more fun in their lives.

The image of a beach ball could mean more than the concept of recreation evident on a surface level. There could be many other possible symbolic meanings associated with this image. What is important for mediums to do is to trust what they feel in relation to the object and, without trying to make the image mean more than it actually does, give out this meaning as chances are they will be completely correct. Perhaps the recipient of the communication has a deceased relative who worked in a factory that produced beach balls or possesses a beach ball given to him or her by a loved one presently in the spirit world. The possibilities are endless. The bottom line for working with symbols is to go with what the image means for you, think outside the box and learn to trust your initial feelings as chances are it will be correct.

Consider the clairvoyant image of a red rose. A red rose certainly might have a different meaning than a yellow rose as colors are significant and have meaning. The majority of people associate a red rose with that of love, romantic or otherwise. There are a few people I have encountered, who relate the image of a red rose with death as such flowers are placed on coffins and displayed at memorial services and funerals. And while there certainly are other interpretations that may be given for this image the concept of romantic or personal love is the most common.

Many mediums when clairvoyantly receiving such an image of a red rose would stop right there and go no further. But when interpreting symbolic imagery, mediums must learn to go beyond the surface level of the image being presented. While it is true that the image of a red rose may indeed mean personal love, it may be also coming from a grandmother in the spirit world named *Rose,* who deeply loved and grew the flower, was born in the month when they bloomed, and had them placed on her coffin at her funeral.

If we examine the stock of the rose we find so many thorns followed by the beautiful petals at the end. Perhaps, the spirit grandmother had an extremely painful and challenging life when she had been in the physical world represented by the thorns and yet there was the conclusion of great healing and the beauty of life indicated by the flower at the end. And perhaps, the recipient of the communication is presently going through the same sort of painful, personal challenges within his or her life, and the message that the spirit grandmother wants to convey is about the healing and resolution that will take place with the recipient and the beauty and blessings of life, despite the hardships. All of the above meaning, both symbolic and literal, can apply to one clairvoyant image.

Misinterpretation does happen with symbolic messages. A medium could see a spirit person surrounded by rabbits and wrongly assume that the man raised the animals, when in reality the last name of the spirit communicator was *Hare.* Think outside the box but don't try to make an image into something that is it not.

Receiving Names Symbolically

Names are not always easy to directly convey, especially since the clairaudient channels of most mediums are not as developed as their ability to receive information through clairvoyance and clairsentience. Besides the name *Rose,* indicated by the images of a rose, other flowers such as daisies, lilies, etc. may represent the names of spirit communicators. Seeing the colors green or brown could indicate that a spirit with the last name of *Green* or *Brown* is coming through. At a mediumship workshop near San Francisco, California, a student medium brought a lion through as part of a spirit message for a Spiritist friend of mine from the Philippines. The lion within itself did not mean anything other than the fact that my friend's last name was *De Leon,* which is Spanish for lion.

Another time, I was demonstrating mediumship at the First Spiritualist Church in Salem, Massachusetts and delivered a message from a spirit grandfather to a man in the congregation. The spirit grandfather showed himself doing carpentry, which I felt had been his occupation and symbolically represented how the spirit was helping his grandson fix some situations in the physical world. I spoke to the recipient after the service who had understood all that I had related. It turns out the recipient worked as a builder and that both the grandfather's and grandson's last names were *Carpenter.*

During a mediumship training weekend, a skeptical investigator, who had previously researched my mediumship, participated in a psychometry exercise, in which students would bring through spirit messages for each other by selecting from a box, a personal object belonging to another member of the group. Another student picked the skeptic's object, a pocket watch, and proceeded to bring through a deceased loved one for the object's owner. Although she did not know that the watch belonged to the skeptic or know anything about him, one of the image's she was shown was a picture of Benjamin Franklin. The skeptic's last name was *Benjamin.*

The spirit aunt of one of my students came through during a private session providing much advice and evidential information. With clairsentience I could intensely feel the character, personality and what her physical build had once been. "She was fuller in her build," I said as I described what I was feeling. This was correct as she had been a larger woman in physical size and her last name was *Fuller* as well. When I received this message I was not aware of the significance of that particular detail, I just verbalized what I intuitively felt while in attunement with the team of spirit helpers. While I did not receive this message in the form of a clairvoyant image, it shows how the spirit personalities working with mediums are able to accurately bring through information when the analytical mind is out-of-the-way.

The logical mind only gets in the way of clear communication from the spirit world. All mediums, regardless of experience, must train themselves, when they find their logical mind beginning to get involved while they are working to instantly push it aside, and verbally express the intuitive flow of ideas and messages coming from the spirit world.

Another time at Cassadaga Spiritualist Camp in Florida, I had three young women come together for a shorter mediumship session. With the first of the three, the spirit operators showed me images of the Southwest part of the United States and I was made aware that she liked this part of the country and physically would do well spending time there. I did not understand at the time why the three young women all found what I was saying to be extremely funny. At the conclusion of the session, they explained to me that they were all flight attendants employed by *Southwest Airlines*.

At a workshop that I attended in at the Lily Dale Assembly in New York, British medium Leonard Young gave the following example in regards to symbolic interpretation. A medium in England during a Spiritualist church service felt drawn to deliver a message to a couple sitting in the back pews. The medium received images of two bells, a bridge, a gate and what appeared to be the end of the bridge. The couple could not relate to what the medium was talking about. The medium spent several minutes trying to figure out the meaning of the message and finally sat down frustrated with his failed efforts.

How would you interpret the images that the medium clairvoyantly received? I have used this example in my mediumship workshops for years and get all sorts of responses from participants in my training programs. The image of two bells many people associate with churches and weddings. A bridge gets you from one side to another and a gate is an entrance to somewhere. The end of the bridge many people interpret to mean the end of something, possibly a life. Someone has physically died and has made the crossing over to the spirit world is a common interpretation. There have been many other interpretations that vigorously analyze and pick apart each of the images. But the correct interpretation was given by another medium, who immediately addressed the same couple after the first medium sat down asking them: "Do you by any chance ever know a *Mr. and Mrs. Bell* who, when they were in the physical world, lived at *Bridgegate End?*" The couple immediately recognized the identities of the spirit communicators and understood the connection.

Over the years I find that symbols are used less in the communications that I receive from the spirit world. While I receive much information visually, I find that much of the ideas and thoughts are conveyed directly through clairsentience and claircognizance without the need for any interpretation.

The main two points to remember with symbols for developing mediums are 1) create your own system or vocabulary with your spirit team and 2) try to expand past the basic interpretations to multi-levels of symbolic and literal meanings for each individual image that is presented.

The following sample symbols and interpretations are examples of images used by my team of spirit helpers to convey information through me. Some of these symbols and their interpretations are extremely basic and generic in nature, but it should provide an idea about how symbology works.

Sample Symbols and Interpretations:

Beach Ball: The recipient needs to play more and have fun.

Bug: Something is disturbing the recipient.

Bunch of Grapes: The recipient needs to rest more and take it easy.

Close Up View of Dirty, Rotted Teeth: The recipient needs to consult a dentist for treatment.

Crystal Ball: The recipient possesses significant mediumistic ability.

Healing Hands Emitting Healing Energy: The recipient is a developed healer who channels healing energies to others.

Hour Glass with Sand: The recipient feels intense anxiety as though they are running out of time.

Light House: The recipient shows the way spiritually or is a source of spiritual strength and guidance for others.

Lighting Bolt hitting the recipient of the message: The recipient of the message is greatly connected and inspired by the power of God that is strongly working through them.

Native American Indian Peace Pipe handed to the recipient: The spirit guides are giving spiritual philosophy and teachings from the spirit world to the recipient to apply in his or her life.

Porcupine with Quills: Getting close to a particular person in the physical world will result in being emotionally hurt through such contact.

Praying Hands with Rosary Beads: The spirit person coming through was a devote Roman Catholic who regularly prayed the rosary.

Raggedy-Ann Doll: A spirit with the name of Ann is coming through for the recipient.

Rainbow: Conditions will be positive and work out.

Red Apple: The recipient needs to go back to school for further education.

Saint Francis of Assisi: The recipient follows the teachings of Saint Francis.

Slow-Moving Tortoise: Like the *Tortoise and the Hare* in *Aesop's Fables* the recipient needs to proceed slowly but steady, instead of rushing, as the results will be positive.

Steam Engine from *The Little Engine that Could* Children's Storybook: The recipient needs to be optimistic and continue with whatever challenges they are facing believing that they can do it.

Sun with Raisins from *Kellog's Raisin Bran* Cereal Box: The recipient feels weak and worn out from physical health problems.

White Medical Uniforms: Spirit doctors are around and working with the recipient for healing.

Exercises for Receiving Names

EXERCISE 31

Names in Telephone Directory

For the development of receiving names using clairvoyance and clairaudience, the practice of looking through the residential section of the telephone directory is an extremely useful method for filling the mind with names that can be utilized by the spirit helpers as part of the messages conveyed to the medium. The more the mind of the medium is familiar with particular names, the easier it will be for such names to be telepathically transmitted and received. To maximize this as an exercise, such study needs to take place regularly for short periods of time.

EXERCISE 32

Names in Baby Book

For the development of receiving first names clairvoyantly, obtaining and studying the contents of a baby book is essential. Students of mediumship should regularly study its content for short periods of time to familiarize themselves with common as well as more unusual names. This way, when such names are stored in the medium's unconscious mind, they will more easily be conveyed by the spirit helpers and received by the medium.

EXERCISE 33

Awareness of People's Names

In order to condition the mind to easily receive names as part of their mediumship, student mediums should try as much as possible to notice the names of people in daily life whom they come in contact with and make a point of learning and addressing them by their names. First names are naturally easier to learn, but efforts to learn and articulate last names, particularly unusual or hard to pronounce ones, should be emphasized as the result will be a mind conditioned to mentally receive similar sounding names conveyed mediumistically.

EXERCISE 34

Awareness of Evidential Details

In order to condition the mind to easily receive details as part of their mediumship, student mediums should imagine individuals they come in contact with in daily life as being spirit communicators and note specifics about their physical features, personality traits or behavior that would make strong evidence mediumistically.

CHAPTER 6

Hearing Spirit

Clairaudience or *clear hearing* is the mental phase of mediumship of psychically hearing sounds communicated by the spirit personalities. There are two types of clairaudience; subjective clairaudience and objective clairaudience.

Subjective Clairaudience

Subjective clairaudience is most commonly experienced by mediums and involves the impression of thoughts in the form of words or other sounds in the mind of the medium. Subjective clairaudient sounds could be names, phrases or sentences, or other sounds such as a dog barking, machinery, or an explosion. While the names of individuals or places may be highly evidential and meaningful for the recipient, the same may be true for other sounds received clairaudiently as well.

Once I was doing a mediumship session for one of my students from my development classes. After saying my opening prayer and tuning in, I heard clairaudiently what sounded like an explosion. This was followed by the mental impression of the name *Bob* and through clairsentience, the physical build and conditions of passing over, of a spirit grandfather, whose personality was very macho like the famous actor John Wayne, and who had left his physical body due to similar health conditions.

The explosion mentally conveyed to me was a *fart* and all of the information, which accurately described the recipient's grandfather fit him to a tee. According to the recipient, he often would deliberately fart in front of members of the family and laugh about it. This one, unusual sound communicated clairaudiently was not only extremely evidential in a factual sense, but also accurately portrayed an important aspect of the personality of the communicator and his distinctive sense of humor.

The sounds through subjective clairaudience are experienced within the inner, intuitive mind of the medium. Clairaudient sounds are also felt and generally accompany information conveyed through clairvoyance and clairsentience. The sounds are loud or soft and the intonation, speech patterns and accent of the spirit voices heard in most cases resemble those of the communicating spirit.

Objective Clairaudience

Although objective clairaudience is the subjective, intuitive experience of the medium, it is termed as such because the sounds heard by the medium resemble sounds heard with the physical ear. In fact, often, it is difficult to tell whether or not the sounds are being heard through objective clairaudience or with the physical ears. The mechanism of objective clairaudience is different than subjective clairaudience in that it involves the use of the mediums etheric body to hear rather than mentally impressed sounds as with subjective clairaudience.

Objective clairaudience is frequently experienced in the sleep state especially in the early morning hours, when the subtle body is partially disconnected from the physical body. In such a receptive condition spirit voices are heard within the medium's mind, personal space, or at a distance. Often, the voices inside the medium's mind sound as though they are spoken through a metallic tube or emitted from a radio at a distance. Frequently, the voices are heard in the area behind and beneath the physical ears. When this happens the medium, deaf to physical sounds, hears only the clairaudient voices which sound toneless and not spoken by a particular gender. In other cases, the voices may be distinct with the accents, speech patterns and intonations of the communicating spirits. The spirit voices at times spontaneously drop into the medium's mind to be verbalized word by word as received, or in some cases the complete verbal message may instantaneously appear

One of the most famous clairaudient mediums in history is the 15th-century heroine, Joan of Arc, who as an uneducated teenage girl, heard the voices of her spirit teachers. Joan of Arc received direction from her guides to lead the French armies in campaigns against the English invaders. The late American medium Arthur Ford was also widely known for his remarkable clairaudient ability. Sir Arthur Conan Doyle, British author of the *Sherlock Holmes* series and prominent advocate for the Spiritualist movement, was greatly impressed by Ford's delivery of evidential spirit messages in London during Ford's visit to England in 1927. Ford describes in his 1958 autobiography *Nothing So Strange,* how Doyle wrote in a British Newspaper: "One of the most amazing things I have ever seen in 41 years of psychic experience was the demonstration of Arthur Ford."

Unlike the majority of mental mediums, who are primarily clairvoyant or clairsentient, Ford's outstanding gift of clairaudience gave him the advantage of being able to directly hear names and other factual information that generally is harder to receive through pictures or feelings. All phases of mediumship have their strengths as well as disadvantages, but when it comes to names clairaudience has a distinct advantage in this regard over the other phases. As noted previously, many times the spirit personalities when working with mediums must convey information in a roundabout way. Not so with clairaudience, as specific names may be directly given to the medium without having to resort to the use of symbology or other means. After Ford's death, serious allegations of fraud were made against him after files containing details about his clients were discovered in his personal belongings. While it would not surprise me if Ford cheated at some points during his career, I have conversed with colleagues of his who describe him as a brilliant medium capable of delivering highly evidential messages.

Many leading platform mediums of the late 19th-century and early 20th-century possessed highly developed clairaudient abilities such as John Slater, who demonstrated his remarkable clairaudience throughout the United States. George Cutter, a noted test medium, would hear the first, middle and last names of the spirit communicators and write them on a blackboard when doing public mediumistic demonstrations.

Self Exercises for Clairaudience

Regular practice of these exercises will enable students to develop their inner hearing by strengthening their clairaudient channels. All mediumship is about establishing a harmonious link and being on the same frequency as the spirit communicators.

EXERCISE 35

Listening with the Conch Shell

Practice using a large conch shell to listen through. Place the shell up to your ears and spend time listening to the sound within.

EXERCISE 36

Paying Attention to Sounds

Pay attention to sounds around you and notice loud and soft differentiation. Practice hearing the sounds within silence. In doing so, the natural clairaudient channels will be awakened.

EXERCISE 37

Projecting Hearing

Practice physically trying to hear by projecting your aural acuity to hear at a distance, inside physical objects or behind objects in proximity or at a distance. Use your physical ears as well as your mind.

EXERCISE 38

Saying "I Hear..."

When delivering spirit messages, whether during a private or group session or a larger public meeting, get into the habit of saying, "I hear" instead of saying, "I see" or " I feel". Emphasize clairaudience even if the information is received through clairvoyance or clairsentience. Doing this will subconsciously program your mind to psychically hear when doing mediumship. This exercise is not meant to endorse dishonesty as complete truthfulness with mediumship is essential. It is not always clear cut which psychic sense is utilized in receiving mediumistic impressions. A medium may say they *see* an image when in reality the idea may have been felt or even just known.

Group Clairaudient Exercises

EXERCISE 39

Clairaudience with Partners

Participants divide into pairs that sit across from each other in two evenly spaced, straight lines. One side works first with clairaudience while the other partner acts as the recipient of the communications. The teacher directs participants in relaxing their physical bodies for the purpose of achieving a deep altered-state and attuning to their team of helpers in the spirit world. Special focus is placed during this meditation on the throat chakra and the area behind and in back of the physical ears. Participants are told to feel as though they have a long, etheric tube connecting from this area to their guides and others in the spirit world, who can directly speak to them through the tube.

Participants are directed to receiving the following information clairaudiently: *a song or music, a name,* and *a phrase* or *words or sentences.* After sharing what they have received. The teacher will direct the participants to receive further information through other psychic means such as clairvoyance or clairsentience which is in turn shared with the recipient. After one side works, the same process is repeated with the roles reserved. After both parties have worked they can give each other feedback. In the manner of musical chairs this exercise may be done multiple times with participants moving to the right after each turn and working with a variety of different partners.

EXERCISE 40

Group Clairaudient Readings

Ask one participant to face the seated group, imagine the etheric tube (Exercise 39) and focus initially to bring through *a name, a song or music* and *a word or sentence.* The participant gives each seated member a clairaudient message containing the required information. This exercise will familiarize the student with the clairaudient channel and enable them to regularly receive information in this manner in the future.

EXERCISE 41

Imagining Sounds

This exercise may be done individually or as part of a group. In this exercise students stimulate their clairaudient abilities by imaging distinct physical sounds. With a group the facilitator should suggest to participants, all of whom are in a deep meditative state, that they imagine loudly hearing within their minds the following sounds:

- *The sound of rain hitting the roof of a car.*
- *A baby crying.*
- *Someone talking in a British accent.*
- *A song by the British music group 'The Beatles'.*
- *A dog barking.*
- *A gong.*
- *Someone talking in a thick 'Southern' accent.*
- *A chainsaw.*

CHAPTER 7

Sensing Spirit

Clairsentience is the phase of mental mediumship in which information from the spirit world is conveyed through sensing and feeling. Most students of mediumship tend to concentrate on the development of clairvoyance. They want to be able to see spirit guides and deceased loved ones and receive spirit messages transmitted visually.

While there is nothing wrong with the desire to receive messages from the spirit world clairvoyantly, a problem develops when student mediums look straight ahead, as though they are wearing blinders, and ignore the data received through their other psychic senses. Remember, clairvoyance is only one form that spirit messages are transmitted and by concentrating too much on upon receiving images, other information may come through, unnoticed, resulting potentially with the message being incomplete or incorrectly interpreted.

Clairsentience reinforces spirit communication received as clairvoyant impressions. The impressions, as individual thought pictures, are often accompanied by a feeling or sense to the overall meaning presented. In this manner, awareness of clairsentient feelings will enable student mediums to better interpret the meaning behind the images, both symbolic and literal, that they are receiving.

Instead of concentrating on receiving images pay attention to what you are feeling in your own body as feelings or such sensations may relate to the features of the communicating spirit's former physical body such as their build, health conditions, manner of passing over, and even specific gestures and mannerisms. If the spirit had been missing a leg, finger or other part of his or her former physical body, an awareness of this fact will be felt by the medium. Obviously, a spirit that was missing a leg in his or her former physical body does not still lack a leg in his or her subtle spirit body. Such information is merely given for the sake of recognition and to provide evidence of the continued existence of the spirit.

As a medium I have psychically sensed the former physical health conditions of many spirits and how they passed over. I have strongly experienced many attributes of the spirit communicators such as feelings in my gums indicative of dental issues or missing my head as result of decapitation.

The body language of the medium is also greatly affected through receiving clairsentience. How many times have you observed a demonstration of mediumship and concentrated completely on listening to the messages being articulated? Body language, gestures and mannerisms channeled through the medium, often convey as much, if not more, information than a verbal message.

Once I was about to give a communication at a Spiritualist church service to a woman, who loudly expressed her recognition of her deceased uncle based on how I was moving my physical body. A former student of mine and practicing professional medium in Massachusetts, once while giving a private session for a client moved his hand to his face in a particular way. This astonished the woman he was working with, who remarked that her grandmother always used to touch her face in the exact same manner.

Overshadowing

Clairsentience as a phase of mediumship leads to overshadowing, in which the personality of the spirit imparts a strong influence within the aura of the medium. When overshadowing takes place the medium goes into a light trance and feels through clairsentience the personality, character and former physical attributes of the spirit communicator. The body language, such as movements and posture, will also reflect that of the overshadowing spirit personality. The consciousness of the medium and that of the spirit communicator gradually blend and the voice pattern, inflection and general manner of speaking, take on characteristics of the spirit communicator. Overshadowing, to the extent the medium is able to let go and step aside, almost always leads to deeper levels of trance and spirit control. The more the medium is able to dis-associate from his or her physical body the more effectively the spirit personality will be able to express him or herself.

With clairsentience the character and personality of the spirit communicator may be completely described in amazingly accurate detail without any visual images received. If the spirit communicator was frequently depressed or suicidal, such intense emotions will be experienced by the medium. Anger, happiness, frustration, it does not matter what the emotion; if it is felt by the spirit personality then the consciousness of the medium will register and express it through clairsentience.

Clairsentience operates primarily through the solar plexus and heart chakras. It is common for people on a purely psychic level to mentally feel the sensations around them. Often times, walking into a crowded place, especially where intoxication or lower consciousness are prevalent, someone who is sufficiently psychically sensitive will automatically react to the negative vibrations when coming in contact with the lower energy.

Before I developed my mediumship my energetic boundaries were vulnerable. I can remember going to social functions where alcohol was being consumed and feeling as though I was kicked in the center of my chest at my heart chakra, or that my solar plexus chakra was tied up in knots. Someone possessing clairsentience, unaware of how to properly psychically protect themselves, may unconsciously react to the energies and psychic atmosphere of the people and places around them.

Psychological and physical conditions, as well as general information, are accurately transmitted through clairsentience. Many mediums receive the bulk of information through clairsentience and little or none through clairvoyance.

Clairsentience Exercises

EXERCISE 42

Sharing Space

I learned a variation of this exercise from the late British teaching medium Eileen Roberts. I have used it countless times over the years and find it highly effective. In this exercise participants should focus exclusively on clairsentience and should specifically try to not use clairvoyance or clairaudience.

The teacher leads participants into a deep altered-state and suggests that they invite one of their main spirit helpers to step forward within their energy field. As soon as they think that they feel the presence of this helper, they should let the teacher know by momentarily raising one hand.

Once all in the group have sensed their helper, the teacher suggests that participants ask that their helper come even closer into their energy field and to again raise their hand when they feel the helpers presence. The teacher suggests that participants request their helper to step back from their energetic space and asks participants to raise a hand when this is felt. Participants may come back briefly from the meditative state and share their experiences with the group.

Next, participants go back into the meditative state and the teacher suggests that they request that another spirit helper come close to them and when they feel the presence to raise their hand. After all have felt the presence of this other helper, the teacher suggests that they invite the helper to come in even closer and that once they feel the presence to raise their hand.

Once this is complete participants may again come back and share their experiences and the difference in feeling experienced between the two spirit helpers. Participants again go back into the meditative state and the teacher suggests that they invite the first helper to once more come in close and when they feel the presence of the helper to raise their hand.

Next, the teacher suggests that they allow the helper to come in even closer than before as though the spirit personality is mentally and energetically blending with them. Participants try to feel the spirit helper literally sharing space as them and sitting in the same seat. As soon as this is felt participants should raise a hand. The character and former physical attributes of the spirit are commonly experienced. The teacher tells the participants to request their helpers to step back from their personal space. At the completion of this exercise participants may come out of the meditative state and share with the group.

This exercise develops awareness of clairsentient information about the spirit communicator including physical features, health conditions, manner of passing, body language and mannerisms as well as character and personality. A deeper altered-state with the medium naturally results from the overshadowing of the spirit within the medium's energy field.

Practice of this exercise will result in improvement in clairsentient awareness and overshadowing and possibly light entrancement. Overall, the regular application of this exercise when working will greatly improve the attunement of the medium by facilitating a deeper level of spirit control.

EXERCISE 43

Overshadowing

Same principles as exercise 42. Participant stands facing group. The teacher suggests the participant allow the spirit to mentally and energetically blend with him or her so that he or she feels as though the spirit is sharing the same space and literally standing in his or her shoes.

The teacher proceeds to suggest to the participant that he or she allows himself or herself to position his or her body like that of the spirit and to move his or her body in the same manner.

This exercise develops clairsentience and overshadowing allowing potentially evidential gestures, mannerisms and overall body language relating to spirits to be displayed by the medium. Allow students to witness the overshadowing process as it evolves and to share their observations.

EXERCISE 44

Sharing Hands

Same principles as exercise 42. Participant stands facing group. Teacher suggests that the participant allows the spirit to mentally and energetically blend with him or her so that he or she feels as though the spirit is sharing the same space and literally standing in his or her shoes.

The participant is instructed to focus his or her awareness upon feeling the hands of the spirit blended with his or her hands. The size and texture of the spirit's hands will be experienced along with a sense of movement relating to physical actions or mannerisms commonly displayed by the spirit during his or her previous physical incarnation. Such movements may relate to professional or personal activities as well as individual traits. The participant may also experience the hands of the spirit holding physical objects that relate in an evidential manner to his or her former physical life.

Chapter 8

Smelling, Tasting and Knowing

Clairalience is the phase of mental mediumship in which smells and aromas are psychically discerned. Usually smells within themselves are not enough to convey the essence of a message or provide complete evidence of survival when received mediumistically. Still, clairalience is an extremely dynamic form of mediumship which provides further detail to the information received through clairvoyance, clairaudience, and clairsentience.

Many times individuals awakening to their intuitive potential psychically perceive odors that others are unable to smell. Aromas belonging to particular spirits, especially when nobody else is able to physically smell them, demonstrate the reality of their presence. The smell of a perfume that a favorite grandmother always wore, cigar smoke as a reminder of a father's lifelong habit, or sage belonging to Native American Indian spirit guardian reassure those in need that they are protected and guided by those in the spirit world.

When working mediumistically from the platform or private session, I commonly receive information utilizing my clairaliance. Smelling cigarette smoke or perfume is not necessarily evidential on its own, but generally reinforces other information received through the other psychic senses.

Once, I was doing a mediumship session for a group of women at the healing sanctuary that I used to run in Massachusetts. The first thing that I received when I tuned in was an extremely disgusting smell. I simultaneously felt as though my belly was larger and that I was wearing an undershirt that had not been changed in a week. I proceeded to describe a father in the spirit world belonging to the women. They instantly recognized him, especially the details about him smelling, as he wore the same shirt for weeks without changing it. People did not like sitting near this individual, and if he sat next to them they would want to get up and move due to the overwhelmingly foul stench emitted by him. The smell of tobacco smoked in cigarettes, cigars and pipes is fairly common to receive. If the spirit communicator regularly smoked marijuana, then it will likely be conveyed through clairailence.

Besides receiving smells mentally through clairalience, there is also a type of physical mediumship in which smells, psychically produced by the spirit chemists, will be detected with the physical nose. Often in group sessions involving physical phenomena odors such as perfumes or incense will be introduced into the seance room. This type of physical phenomena is objective in nature as everyone present will experience the manifestations through their physical senses. The physical production of smells is completely different from clairsalience as with the former it is subjective in nature and dependent upon the medium's mental attunement with the communicating spirit people.

The late Ted Fricker, a well-known British Spiritualist healer, made use of his clairalience ability when treating patients. The spirit doctors working through him made him psychically smell distinct odors for the physical ailments of his patients. While I have met many mediums able to diagnosis health conditions psychically through seeing, hearing or sensing, Fricker is the only medium, I have ever heard about using smell for that purpose.

Psychic Taste Buds

Clairgustance is the psychic ability to taste impressions transmitted from the spirit world. Over the years as a medium, I have psychically tasted many things such as rotting teeth and gum disease as well as chewing tobacco. Foods are the most common tastes conveyed mediumistically.

The foods presented by the spirit communicators are generally the foods associated with them that they prepared or enjoyed. Information received through psychically tasting, while incomplete within itself in terms of providing evidence of survival or higher guidance, reinforces information psychically received through the other senses.

Instant Awareness

Claircognizance or *clear knowing* is the psychic ability to receive ideas or information instantly with full understanding. With claircognizance the medium will often not even be aware that they have received the communication and yet the idea or understanding will strongly be known. Unlike the symbolic images received clairvoyantly, there is no interpretation necessary or lag time in receiving the messages conveyed, which results in the meaning of the messages correctly conveyed without misinterpretation or embellishment on the part of the medium. Claircognizance many times functions by providing the instant interpretation and meaning to the clairvoyant images conveyed. It also often fills in the gaps of other information received through clairvoyance, clairaudience and clairsentience by enabling the medium to receive important details immediately.

Clairaliance/Clairgustance/Musical Chairs Exercises

EXERCISE 45

Opening Up from Heart to Share

Participants line up in two straight rows facing each other holding hands. The teacher guides the group in a short meditation for relaxation and focusing on the unconditional love in the heart chakra at the center of the chest. Participants concentrate on sending love and healing from their hearts to their partners across from them. The energy will be felt through the arms and hands and especially as a beam between the heart centers of partnered pairs. Upon completion and coming back from the meditative state participants are ready to work in bringing through information for each other.

EXERCISE 46

Smelling and Tasting With Partners

Participants pair up facing each other in two straight lines and begin by holding hands and taking turns with the following exercise. The teacher suggests that the participants working initially only focus on receiving *a smell* and *a taste* for their partner. After this is done and shared with their partner as well as the group, the teacher suggests that the participant bring through a spirit personality with messages connected to the smell and taste.

After working the results are shared with the group and feedback given by the recipient. The recipient should never volunteer information or provide feedback while receiving, as educationally it is important for student mediums be kept in the dark in order that they develop confidence in themselves and in the spirit source of their information.

After one side works, the exercise is repeated with the other side.

In musical chair fashion, this exercise is repeated, with one side or both sides switching chairs and partners by physically moving to the right.

EXERCISE 47

Musical Chairs

Participants face partners in two straight lines holding hands. Taking turns, partners bring through spirit communicators using all means of communication. Partners may switch partners by moving to the right.

EXERCISE 48

Speed Drill Timed Musical Chairs

Participants face partners in two straight lines holding hands. Only one side works in this exercise with other side acting as recipients for the communications. The participants working mediumistically remain stationary, while the other side composed of recipients moves to the right at the signal of the teacher. Participants attempt to bring through spirit personalities and messages for each partner sitting in front of them. At the signal of the teacher, those working as mediums break their connection and those acting as recipients move to the right. The teacher may time this drill in two-minute increments. Speed drills in the fashion of musical chairs enable students to develop the ability to change vibrations and bring through information quickly and directly.

EXERCISE 49

Imagining Smells

The teacher leads participants into a deep meditative state and leaving short intervals between suggests a series of smells be imagined. Smells such as;

- *fresh bread*
- *rotten fish*
- *turpentine*
- *lavender*
- *fresh rain*
- *cigar smoke*
- *mothballs*

Additional smells may be included as well. At the end participants may provide feedback.

EXERCISE 50

Imagining Tastes

As in exercise 49, the teacher leads participants into a deep meditative state and leaving short intervals between suggests a series of tastes be imagined. Tastes such as;

- *carrots*
- *baked potato*
- *garlic*
- *chocolate*
- *roast beef*
- *brandy*
- *salt*
- *vinegar*

Additional tastes may be included as well. At the end participants may provide feedback.

CHAPTER 9

Trance Channeling

Inspirational mediumship takes place with people from all walks of life, most of whom have never heard of the concept of mediumship. When ordained ministers speak from their hearts, the sincerity and deep conviction of their words and energy potentially attract outside influences to work through them. The same is true with artists or musicians expressing themselves creatively. Clairvoyant observation of the aura of a good speaker throughout his or her address reveals the extent of the external spirit influence while he or she speaks. The strong presence within the energy fields will be apparent.

Inspirational speaking may involve only a few ideas originating outside of the mediums mind that will be articulated with the medium's vocabulary and manner of speaking. The medium's mind is involved with any form of inspirational mediumship and affects the quality of the material transmitted through the process. The educational background, vocabulary, and experience of a speaker influences the quality of the inspirational speaking. Spirit personalities express themselves through instruments of like background. An intellectually oriented address would best be expressed through a medium on a similar wavelength.

Light Trance

Inspirational mediumship is a light trance state gradually induced by the controlling spirit personalities. The control and distinct changes of the medium's manner of speaking are apparent as the medium enters into a deeper altered-state. Inspirational medumship is not limited to speaking as many artists and musicians receive in varying degrees inspiration from the spirit world.

Spirit control with inspirational medium may consist of five percent the spirit and 95 percent the medium. The minds of the medium and the spirit blend to create a composite of both personalities. As the medium gradually descends into a deeper altered-state-of-consciousness, less of his or her mind is involved as increasingly more of the spirit is expressed. Spirit control of the medium's central nervous system results in manipulation of the medium's physical movements and speech. The medium experiences a flow of thought containing ideas expressed verbally, artistically or musically and feels as though he or she is standing is the presence of a higher power. Mediums need to simply express the ideas without trying to analyze the content. Any involvement on the part of the medium will interrupt the flow of thought and sever the delicate connection.

In the beginning stages of trance development, often, the control is incomplete due in part to the medium's resistance and inability to let go and the spirit's ability to exert sufficient influence. The volume of the medium's voice during the channeling may need adjustment with both the spirit and medium making an effort not to speak too softly or loudly.

Clairvoyance and inspirational speaking, often, progressively lead to deeper levels of control, during which the medium's voice pattern, inflection, and overall manner of speech change to reflect that of the spirit communicator. Watch out for mediums embellishing their trance mediumship with phony accents and unnecessary theatrics. Generally such displays have more to do with the medium, and what the medium unconsciously thinks he or she should sound like, than the spirit communicator.

Innocent Delusion

For example, I attended an open house at an educational institution in San Francisco, California and heard a practicing channeler talk about her psychic unfoldment and how she began to bring through spirit guides. According to her, when she started to channel, she received information from the 155th plane in the spirit world. After several years of channeling she began to bring through information from even higher guides that lived on the 567th plane. She elaborated in detail how, during the process of channeling, her guides would contort her body like a *pretzel* positioning her legs behind her head. Another medium in the UK believed that he had a spirit alligator as a guide and would lie on the floor and wiggle forward during his channeling sessions. It is very easy to mix the imagination with genuine spirit messages and not be able to tell the difference. Sadly, many displays of trance mediumship are either fake or delusion.

How to Discern Authentic Entrancement

What do you feel energetically while the channeling is taking place? It is a good exercise to clairvoyantly assess medium's in the process of channeling. The spirit communicator and energies are discernible within the expanded aura of the medium.

Does the channeled information convey facts or ideas beyond that of the medium's mentality? Genuine channeled material demonstrates a superior, spiritual intelligence at work separate from the consciousness of the medium. Flowery words and platitudes are unnecessary as spiritual truth is straight forward and to the point.

Does the pattern of speech during the channeling flow? It is evident when entrancement takes place as the medium's speech pattern changes with an overall different sentence structure and use of grammar. Information truly channeled from the spirit world flows with no time for breaks or interference from the mind of the medium. A good talk is well-organized, original and provides comprehensive insight. Responses to questions should be instant without hesitation. Unnecessary pauses indicate that the medium's mind is not out of the way.

Are there measurable physiological changes? An entranced medium exhibits a lower body temperature, slower heart rate and pattern of breath, and no rapid-eye-movements or REM and also experiences less reaction to physical pain and touch. The eyes of the medium also tear slightly after returning from trance to regular consciousness. Many Filipino trance mediums I know cry when channeling as they take on the emotions of the spirit communicators.

The Needle Test

The medium's lack of response to physical stimuli may be measured by inserting needles into the body. In rural China and Indonesia there are mediums who insert multiple, long sharp needles into their tongues and other parts of the body while entranced. The mediums, of course, register no pain during this experience as they are functioning in a deep altered-state fully protected by the controlling spirit influences.

An experienced medium I knew in Massachusetts once received a phone call from the proprietor of a metaphysical bookstore, she was concerned that some attendees went into trance while in the circle that took place in her shop. Unsure of what to do, she contacted him for advice about how to properly handle the situation. The medium, being quite confrontational and aggressive in nature, showed up the next week at the meditation class, and holding a very long and sharp hairpin addressed the group: "I understand that some of you have been going into trance. This is very interesting. We are going to have to document the depth of your trance." None of the people who had allegedly gone into trance the week before did so that evening and none came back.

I told the above story at a mediumship workshop that I was teaching at a Spiritualist center in Akreyuri, Iceland. An experienced Icelandic medium remarked that he once had broken his hand and while heavily bandaged, his spirit guide had requested participants, at a seance that he was conducting, to grab one of his fingers and pull. As one of the participants complied with the guide's request, he was told by the spirit that he was not pulling hard enough and needed to yank the fingers even more. The participant followed the guide's instructions and upon coming out of trance, the medium did not feel any pain or discomfort with his broken fingers.

T. Jack Kelly, a dynamic platform medium at the Lily Dale Assembly in New York, regularly demonstrated blindfold billet mediumship under the control of his helpers. A longtime resident of Lily Dale, who observed Kelly working back in the 1940's on the platform of the Lily Dale Auditorium recounted to me the time that Kelly's spirit control took a hairpin and forcefully stuck it into Kelly's forehead. Next, the control requested a large man seated in the audience to come up on the platform and pull it out. The man responded to the guide's request, yet was unable to remove it from the forehead of the medium. The control then remarked that the man was not using enough force and proceeded to pull it out.

Never Touch the Entranced Medium

It is important to note that while a medium in a deeper level of trance will not register physical pain, unless permission is granted by the spirit control, they should never be touched under any circumstances. Unrestricted touch when the medium is in an altered-state-of-consciousness is potentially hazardous for the medium, especially during sessions involving the use of ectoplasm for producing physical phenomena.

A friend of mine did a trance address at Spiritualist church in the UK and at the conclusion of his talk, the chairperson reached over and took hold of his arm to assist him back to his seat. This unexpected action greatly shocked the medium and left large welt-like burns at the location of contact.

Training for Entrancement

In most cases, the development of trance channeling is gradual and takes years for the spirit teachers to prepare their candidate for actual entrancement. The medium may first develop and practice other phases of mediumship such as clairvoyance or healing before the level of control is strengthened. The state of trance is different from entrancement as trance does not involve spirit control.

Many mediums are unaware of their natural ability and are taken over by the spirit personalities without having any idea of what is happening. This is not the preferred approach for development, but it serves the immediate purpose of developing suitable channels for proving to the world that life continues after physical death.

Maurice Barbanell, the late British journalist and founder of the Spiritualist weekly newspaper *Psychic News*, thought the idea of mediumship was complete rubbish when he attended a London seance at the age of 19. At this first seance a medium told him that he would develop mediumship, a message he considered ridiculous. The next week he returned to the group and ended up controlled by a spirit teacher named Silver Birch, who spoke spiritual philosophy through him for the next 61 years.

The late Maude Chalfant, an elderly medium, I knew in at the Church of Two Worlds in Washington, DC, like Barbanell, was similarly, unexpectedly, entranced at a home seance she attended by chance when she thought she was going to a Bible study. Chalfant knew absolutely nothing about mediumship or psychic phenomena. As a result of this startling experience, Chalfant learned how to properly work with her mediumship.

Undoubtedly, both Barbanell and Chalfant possessed considerable potential for entrancement. Although gradual development is best, in some cases, such as described, the spirit world will entrance their candidate by surprise. My teacher Sylvia Giunta sat in a development circle weekly for five years before entrancement took place and received personal tutoring from an experienced trance medium for several years before she publicly demonstrated trance channeling.

Common Misconceptions

There are many misconceptions regarding entrancement perpetuated by many mediums out of ignorance or the desire to appear psychically powerful. As previously noted, the personalities of both the medium and the spirit control blend to energetically create a composite personality. This is an important fact to recognize as many people think that once the medium is controlled that the medium is unconscious and totally unaware of what is taking place. The mind of the medium always to some extent exerts an influence over the content of the channeled information. Many people also wrongly believe that the spirit enters the physical body of the medium when in reality the spirit works through the aura.

Deep Trance

Deep trance is an extremely rare phase of mediumship. In most cases of entrancement the medium is consciously aware of the words they are speaking. Mediums may partially dislocate from their physical bodies, aware of their voice speaking, but unable to interfere as the words are expressed. The spirit may also speak foreign or ancient languages, unknown to the medium and others present.

In deeper levels of full-trance mediums may experience out-of-body travel and observe their physical body from a distance or even travel into the spirit world. Although the consciousness of the medium is completely submerged with the medium unaware of what is taking place, even in levels of deep trance the medium's mind is involved in the process. Spirit teachers explain that the mind of the medium is often a challenge to work through due to the medium's beliefs, prejudices, and tendencies to think along certain lines.

Deep trance often leads to physical mediumship, in which the spirit operators create physical manifestations utilizing the psychic force found within the medium. The medium may be placed in a deep or *dead* trance during which ectoplasm may be drawn from the body for the production of physical phenomena. There are deep trance mediums used by the spirit controls to handle hot coals and similarly heated objects.

Obstacles

The biggest obstacles to the development of trance originate within the mind of the medium. First and foremost is the tendency that most people have have of wanting to be in control. A tense mind that refuses to let go, results in a tense body with mental blocks, which effectively prevents control from taking place. Unnecessary fear or inhibitions, conscious or unconscious, also need to be eradicated for without complete trust in the spirit operators, entrancement will not be achieved.

Trance is a natural process which cannot be forced. In many indigenous cultures, trance states are induced through physical movement, singing and music, which allow the medium, free from inhibitions, to spontaneously attain an altered-state-of-consciousness. Students of mediumship conditioned by modern, materialistic culture lack such spontaneity and generally possess mental blocks that prevent entrancement from taking place.

Another major block is that the medium will often doubt the information that is coming through, uncertain if the ideas or words expressed originate from the spirit world or his or her own imagination. It is more important for the student medium to speak without worrying about accuracy or how much of the content originates from the spirit personality and how much is a product of his or her own mind.

It is completely natural for the mediums to hear themselves speaking as it is their vocal chords that the spirit personalities are utilizing. Mediums with less experience think they are not actually channeling and let their own minds get in the way. The novice medium should vocalize what he or she feels is coming through even if just one word or sentence originates from the spirit world.

The ability to mentally disassociate from the physical body and external environment is a quality essential for trance channeling. While most people are capable of developing mediumship, few possess the ability to sufficiently let go for entrancement to take place.

I knew a trance medium who began seeing a therapist to work on personal issues that were preventing her from moving forward. The therapy brought much-needed clarity into her life along with terrifying recollections of sexual abuse and molestation by close members of her family as a small child.

The childhood sexual abuse experienced by this medium enabled her to effectively disassociate from her external environment and physical body. In this case, the disassociation provided a means to shield her innocent mind from the extreme trauma inflicted upon her. Naturally, the ability to mentally detach assisted her unfoldment as a medium and especially with her development as a trance channel

What does the medium feel while undergoing the process of entrancement? Mediums experiencing entrancement may feel a number of different physical or energetic sensations as the controlling spirits blend with them through the aura. Tightness and constriction in the area of the throat are common sensations along with feelings of faintness or losing consciousness.

With the deepening of the meditative state a medium feels as though he or she is losing consciousness and that the upper part of his or her physical body is expanding. This feeling of expansion is common and may lead to an even greater loss of physical sensation and disassociation from the physical body.

Spirit communicators are able to control the central nervous system and voice box of the entranced medium. A medium under spirit control feels his or her mouth and vocal chords utilized to speak and hears the words automatically spoken, but is unable to interfere.

The frequency of vibrations involved in trance channeling is much faster and stronger than the vibrations of the physical world. At times depending upon the energy and level of the communicator the information channeled through the medium may be transmitted extremely quick with much enthusiasm and force.

Temperature changes are also apparent with intense warmth experienced as control takes place. Psychic breezes of extreme chilliness are also felt within the atmosphere of the seance room and around the medium. Such psychic breezes are generally associated with trance and the production of physical phenomena.

The late British medium Horace Leaf, who lectured and taught mediumship in many countries around the world, describes the medium's experiences undergoing the process of entrancement.

> *The oncoming of spirit-control is fairly well-known. The medium may feel pressure about his forehead or on top of his head; he may feel as if his hair were being lightly ruffled; or he may feel a local or general lowering of temperature; his heart may beat rapidly and his breath become spasmodic. As a rule, these symptoms are followed by definite physical reactions. His hands may involuntarily clasp or unclasp, his head turn or roll from side to side; or his whole body*

may tremble. These and similar reactions are reliable signs that spirit-control is taking place.

If the medium is of the unconscious order, the loss of consciousness will in all probability take place in one of two ways. Either his consciousness will seem gradually to decrease until it becomes like a "point of light" and then blank out; or he may become more and more drowsy until he falls into what seems to be an ordinary sleep. In both cases the body is liable gradually to lose muscular tone, settling into what may be described as a physical lethargy. This is invariably a good sign.

There may, however, be a reverse action and the condition known as catatonia manifest. In this case the medium becomes contorted, his muscles grow extremely tense and contracted, causing, in its most advanced form, his legs and arms to be crooked and body bent. There is usually a gradual leading up to this over a prolonged period involving many sittings.

There is no need for fear, as the cause of the condition is well known and perfectly natural. It is occasioned by the instinct of self-preservation resisting the wishes of the medium to subordinate his consciousness to that of the invading spirit. The instinct of self-preservation naturally endeavors to maintain the normal individuality; this causes a conflict with the medium's will, and the catatonia is the physical expression of this interesting psychological state. In course of time the instinct yields to the will and the contortions slowly decrease until finally they appear to cease. No doubt, however, these conditions are present in every case of spirit-control, although they may be so faint and slurred over as not to be noticeable.[1]

Impersonation, in which the medium intensely experiences the personality, character, and sensations relating to the controlling spirit's physical death and other attributes, commonly takes places during entrancement. Mediums may impersonate multiple spirits during a session as they are overshadowed and controlled by various communicators. Often, the controlling spirits impress the medium's mind with vivid memories of their former physical lives and deaths. It is important for mediums to remain detached and undisturbed by such sensations. A disciplined medium is always in control of his or her mediumship and is unaffected by such communications.

Spirit Controls

Spirit teachers spend considerable time learning how to channel through their medium. One or two spirits commonly speak through the entranced medium and in many cases serve as intermediaries for other spirits who lack the skill to directly come through. Often, it is a group of spirit teachers who express their collective voice through a given channel and even a singular spirit teacher generally represents many more in the spirit world.

Channeling may be performed standing or sitting. The spirit control may connect with the medium from behind, above, in front, or from the sides depending upon the situation. The chair used by the medium for channeling preferably is one with adequate back support and arms to support the medium while entranced. Mental tenseness, anxiety, and physical discomfort interfere with the process of entrancement. Channeling standing up is especially powerful for connecting with the spirit world as the psychic energies along the spinal column and chakra system are fully aligned.

The environment used for development of entrancement needs to be free from distractions and noise. Phones naturally should be silenced as loud noise greatly interferes with student mediums being able to deepen their levels of trance. An experienced entranced medium will be unaffected by external noises, but for the novice intrusive sounds are a distraction that are detrimental for inducing a deepened trance state.

The development of trance ideally should take place in a circle facilitated by an experienced trance medium or through the one-on-one assistance of a qualified teacher, who provides energetic support and verbal feedback. Entrancement generally should not be attempted alone, although students of trance should practice deeper altered-states-of-consciousness during their own personal meditations as well as when sitting in the development circle. It is always good during entrancement to have someone present, who understands the process and is able to provide support.

Once entrancement has commenced questions may be directed to the controlling spirit personalities about their identity, purpose in coming through, and messages they wish to convey. Speaking to the control directly assists the spirit in the process of coming through. When the session needs to be brought to a close, the spirit may be encouraged to release control of the medium. Upward sweeping motions to the aura of the medium help bring the medium back to regular consciousness as does snapping the fingers. The medium may also be instructed to come back. When addressing either the spirit control or the medium the words must be directly spoken with authority.

Methods to Induce Entrancement

Different methods work better for different mediums. Mediums should experiment with the following basic methods and see what works best for them. These methods may be applied separately or combined. The Spiritualist approach to achieving entrancement is passive and involves the medium quieting the mind and progressively relaxing the physical body. Other approaches such as those practiced within indigenous cultures actively involve movement, song, and ceremony. The main objective is to disengage the mind of the medium in such away that an altered-state-of-consciousness is induced, which allows for spirit control to take place.

Deep Breathing

It is helpful for mediums during the process of entrancement to concentrate on their breath and as much as possible let their minds disassociate from their physical bodies. In order to better induce an altered-state-of-consciousness the medium must learn to master the skill of breathing deeply into the lower abdomen while consciously relaxing his or her physical body. The muscles of the face, tongue and throat need to be especially relaxed.

Guided Imagery and Verbal Instruction

Verbal instructions and guided meditation also assist the process of entrancement. It is beneficial for a qualified medium to guide the medium using suggestion and imagery into a trance state. The assisting medium may also speak directly to the medium and the controlling spirit to provide encouragement in making the process take place as smoothly as possible.

Sound Vibration

Soft, meditative music is amazingly effective as a tool for induction of the trance state. The only drawback to music is that the medium may become dependent on particular pieces that are frequently used. It should not become a crutch relied upon by the medium.

The singing and chanting of mantras, prayers and spiritual songs is especially powerful for trance work and can effectively be combined with physical movement and dance. In many cultures and religious traditions this approach is utilized. Drumming and the use of other musical instruments is also an effective method for trance induction.

Mesmeric Passes

Auric passes or sweeps from the top of the medium's head down the physical body calm the nervous system and induce a deeper altered-state-of-consciousness as do downward stroking motions that make gentle contact with the medium's physical body. Such physical actions are best performed by another medium experienced with the process of trance.

Movement

Whirling Dervishes, Shamanic Healers, the Shakers, *Bhakti* Yoga Practitioners and many other traditions use dance and movement to induce spiritual ecstasy, altered-states-of-consciousness and in some cases spirit control. Movement is natural and easily leads to disassociation from the physical body. Indigenous mediums worldwide use dance as a means of connecting with the spirit world.

Trance Exercises

EXERCISE 51

Inducing Entrancement Seated

The medium should sit comfortably with both arms and legs uncrossed. The teacher uses both hands to make long downward passes from the top of the head down the body. This motion soothes the mind of the medium and energetically facilitates the blending of the spirit personality with that of the medium. An outward energetic pulling motion may be made from the solar plexus area of the medium. Generally, energy is drawn from this area during mediumistic work and this motion further facilitates the trance state and entrancement by the spirit control.

The teacher acts as a battery and uses their hands to direct energy around the medium especially the areas of the head, face and throat. If necessary, it may be helpful for other batteries, positioned behind and at either side of the seated medium, to assist with the process. A horseshoe configuration is ideal for this purpose as those seated in front of the medium naturally provide energy. The medium should not be physically touched by anyone, unless directed to do so by the spirit control.

The teacher gently verbally encourages the medium to relax and get out-of-the-way. Relaxation should especially be induced in the mediums upper body as well as facial muscles and tongue. The teacher should encourage the spirit to speak by firmly and directly asking questions, and intuitively sense how to proceed in terms of verbally and energetically facilitating entrancement.

At the conclusion of the session, the teacher should ask the spirit to release the medium and make sweeping, energetic passes from the feet of the medium, up the body and over the head. The teacher should also verbally direct the medium to gently and gradually return to regular consciousness. It is important to give the medium fresh water to drink and time to fully come back. The medium, teacher and other participants should share their experiences and observations with the group.

EXERCISE 52

Inducing Entrancement Standing

The participant stands with hands resting on chair placed in front of them for support. The same principles as detailed in Exercise 51 for induction into the trance state are applied by the teacher. Channeling in the standing position is powerful as the energies are in better alignment.

EXERCISE 53

Disassociation for Entrancement

Participants stand with their hands resting on a chair for support. Teacher leads participants on a short meditation to relax the physical body. Participants envision themselves completely standing in the center of two energetic spheres. One sphere extends from their body about the distance of the ceiling above their heads and the second sphere extends even further in distance.

After entering into an altered-state-of-consciousness participants envision a spiral of energy moving down from the top of their heads through their spinal columns and out the bottom of their feet into the earth.

Next, participants mentally extend their awareness to the edge of the first sphere on their left side. This is followed by moving awareness to the second sphere on their left before returning to the center. The process is repeated by moving awareness to both spheres on the right side, behind, and above.

Participants will experience varying degrees of disassociation from their physical bodies. Sensations of expansion and spinning are common experiences. This exercise is an excellent tool for achieving the disassociation necessary for entrancement.

Inspirational Speaking Exercises

EXERCISE 54

Common Object

Instructor places common object such as a soda can in front of the group. After a short meditation each member of the group stands up in front and gives an inspirational address influenced by the object regarding a spiritual concept. Each participant must speak for at least two minutes minimum.

EXERCISE 55

Angel Cards

Instructor places turned over, illustrated angel cards or similar inspirational illustrations at the feet of the participants. Participants take turns standing and picking up the card and speaking on the subject that relates to the card for a minimum length of two minutes.

The individual card given to each participant is also a personal message for him or her.

---

1 Horace Leaf, *What Mediumship Is*, London, UK, Psychic Press, 1938., pp.138-139.

CHAPTER 10

Automatic Writing and Spirit Art

Automatic writing is both a mental and physical phase of mediumship, in which the medium's arm and hand will be controlled completely by the spirit personalities for the purpose of writing or producing artistic works through painting or drawing. The speed of the writing is considerable and may be produced with the medium in varying degrees of consciousness from fully awake to a light or completely deep trance state.

Writings produced automatically may be written in a style and manner completely different from that of the medium. The writings may contain evidential facts and information about subjects unknown to the medium. In some cases the automatic scripts may be written in foreign or ancient languages unknown to the medium and others present. The scripts may be written upside down or backwards and require the use of a mirror for viewing. Automatic control may take place with both the mediums arms and even both feet being simultaneously being controlled. While the writing is taking place the mediums mind may be focused elsewhere with the medium engaged in a conversation with others.

The late Chico Xavier, a famous Brazilian medium, produced hundreds of published books including many bestsellers created by means of automatic writing. Stainton Moses, a 19th-century British medium, authored through automatic writing the classic *Spirit Teachings,* containing higher spiritual philosophy, as well as several other works.

When automatic painting or drawing takes place the works of art are produced at rapid speed. The medium does not have to possess any artistic skill whatsoever with this type of mediumship. The works done in a short amount of time may be extremely developed at a level of refinement comparable to finished artistic works completely by a skilled artist over a longer period of time.

The Brazilian trance medium Jose Medrado is one such medium who automatically paints at great speeds while under the control of great master artists such as Monet, Van Gogh, Renoir and others. The spirit artists are able to control Medrado and simultaneously rapidly produce works from four separate spirit artists in four distinct styles using all the hands and feet of the medium. The completed works resemble that of each spirit master working through him.

There are two approaches that the spirit operators will work in controlling the movements of the medium for the purpose of producing the writing or art. The first involves a strong degree of control which acts upon the central nervous system and unconscious mind of the medium. The mediums mind, although consciously not involved, may still with this approach as with automatic speaking or trance channeling affect the content of the works being produced automatically. Automatic writing can be classified as both a mental and physical phase of mediumship. It is mental because the mind of the mental must be in proper attunement and may be at some stages involved with the content of what is being written. The spirit chemists may also create an ectoplasmic arm over the arm of the medium for the purpose of controlling and directing its movements. Due to the mechanism involved with such control and the use of ectoplasm such an approach would be classified as a physical phase of mediumship.

Spirit Art

Spirit or psychic art like automatic writing is both a mental and physical phase of mediumship. Spirit art may be fully impressional with the medium rendering portraits of the deceased that have been mentally received through clairvoyance or clairsentience. Spirit art may also be produced under more direct levels of control, in which the spirit artists will produce the portraits at a considerable quicker speed than a similar portrait done by an artist working non-mediumistically. The British medium Frank Leah was a brilliant psychic artist, who would complete finished works of recognizable spirit personalities in a matter of minutes. Coral Polge was another prominent British psychic artist, whose works were extremely evidential in depicting realistic renditions of deceased personalities.

It is helpful for the development of psychic portraiture that the medium possess a basic understanding of the shape and proportion as well as technical skill. Rita Berkowitz, a psychic artist from Massachusetts and co-author along with Debra Romaine of *The Complete Idiot's Guide to Communicating with Spirits*, has taught fine art professionally on a college level and holds a Masters of Fine Art degree. Her works, when placed side by side with actual photographs of the spirit communicators, are excellent examples of what may be achieved evidentially with this type of mediumship. I have heard about a New Zealand medium from many years ago, who sculpted the facial features of the communicating spirit personalities using modeling clay.

Students of mediumship who want to develop the ability to produce images of spirit personalities should not worry too much about their level of artistic proficiency. Many so-called psychic artists render portraits of angels and guides connected to the recipients of their work. As beautiful as such works may be, since they do not depict portraits of distinct personalities that may be identified, they possess little, if any, evidential value. Student mediums should develop the skill of producing portraits of recognizable deceased personalities as such works strongly demonstrate the reality of life after death.

Automatic Writing and Spirit Art Exercises

EXERCISE 56

Automatic Writing

Participants sit in a deep meditative state with a hand holding a pen positioned to write on paper or both hands with fingers positioned to type on a computer keyboard. Mentally invite the spirit control to come closer and allow his or her energy to energetically and mentally blend. Especially feel as though the hands of the spirit personality are overshadowing the physical arms and hands of the medium. The medium should be in a state of disassociation from the physical body and allow the spirit control to convey messages that are manually written or typed with a keyboard. This exercise may also be used in a similar manner for the development of controlled drawing or painting.

EXERCISE 57

Drawing Auric Colors

Participants mentally attempt to see and feel the energy field of a partner seated in front of them. With paper and colored crayons, oil pastels, chalk or markers, participants depict the colors and energies that they perceive boldly and brightly on a sheet of paper. Oil pastels are extremely good for psychic art-the colors are rich, blend, malleable, and so good for expressive, fluid work. The end result can be much more gratifying, especially for non-artists, to allow color and impression to come through. Detail is not so important for this exercise as much as brightness and dynamic application of color and form. Participants should attempt to fill the whole page and not worry too much about artistic perfection or detail. The more messy and expressive the better. After everyone in the group has completed their illustration, participants may take turns showing their work to the group and explaining their interpretation of what they have depicted. A number of participants may take turns sitting in front of the group with the exercise repeated.

EXERCISE 58

Drawing Spirit Personalities in the Aura

In the manner described in the previous exercise, participants use color to depict the energy fields of a participant sitting in front of the group. Participants should also mentally ask to be shown spirit communicators around the subject sitting in front of them. Participants may see or sense colored lights, transparent forms or masses of energy, as well as distinct faces or forms of spirit personalities. Participants should work general to specific in terms of their depictions. While detail is fine in this exercise, it should be included after completing the basic form and colors associated with the spirit personality.

Once everyone in the group has finished participants may take turns sharing with their work with the recipient and the rest of the group. After all have finished sharing, the recipient may provide feedback. A number of participants may take turns sitting in front of the group and the exercise repeated.

EXERCISE 59

Cartoon Spirit

Participants pair up, facing each other sitting in chairs. After the teacher leads a short guided meditation participants tune in and attempt to see the facial features of a spirit personality connected with their partners. Instead of attempting to draw a realistic representational portrait, participants should draw a caricature or cartoon of the head and facial features of the spirit personality. Line and color should equally be emphasized in this exercise. After both parties have spent ample time completing their works, they should share their art with each other along with any other impressions they have received. Feedback may be given as well.

Not everyone possesses artistic ability. Drawing a cartoon illustration of the spirit personality frees up potential anxieties or inhibitions that the medium might have about his or her lack of artistic ability and allows him or her to concentrate on depicting the main features of the personality presenting themselves from the spirit world.

EXERCISE 60

Spirit Portraiture Representational Drawing

Note, for this exercise it is helpful for participants to have at least a basic idea of anatomical proportions for the face and head as well as some drawing skills. Participants pair up, facing across from their partner. After a short meditation they tune in and attempt to see and feel a spirit personality connected to their partner. Taking the time necessary to complete the portrait, participants should work general to specific and utilize the entire page. First, the form of the head should be rendered, followed by more specific line work or detail. Once both partners have completed their portraits, they should take turns sharing with each other their work and any other impressions that they may have received.

EXERCISE 61

Spirit Fashion

Participants pair up, with partners seated across from them. After a short meditation, they tune in and attempt to see and feel the form of the spirit personality connected with their partners. Emphasis in this exercise should be upon drawing the clothing and adornments of the spirit personality. The type of clothing indicates much in terms of evidence about the communicator, including potentially the time period they lived in the physical world, occupation, social class, etc. Participants should utilize the entire page in making their depictions and work as boldly and colorfully as possible. After participants have completed their works, they may share with each other along with any other impressions received. Feedback at this time may also be given.

CHAPTER 11

Structure

Mental discipline is essential for quality mediumship. A disciplined medium is able to mentally detach from his or her external surroundings, attune to the spirit world and receive accurate spirit communications. Most students of mediumship do not achieve this skill overnight and are easily distracted by their own thoughts as well as conditions around them. When it comes to any form of education, the mind works best with structure and organization. Mediumship is no different as the process involved is a cooperative effort between the medium and the team of spirit helpers. Regular sitting for development in circle as well as daily periods for personal meditation and prayer must be strictly observed. Lack of proper discipline in mediumship training and the personal life of the medium leads to sloppy, unreliable mediumship.

The structure and organization necessary for quality mediumship are not only necessary for the training of the medium, but are absolute requirements for the communications mentally transmitted by the spirit team to the receptive medium. If the structure of a communication conveyed by the spirit team is organized with the same pattern for the content each time, it will make it easier for all parties involved in the learning process. It will be easier for the spirit team to transmit and for the medium to receive. The efficiency of carefully transmitted telepathic messages from the spirit world to the receptive mind of the medium only improves and expands through regular, disciplined training and constant practice. An organized message is also easier and less confusing for the recipient of such a spirit communication to understand.

There are a variety of formulas taught by different mediumship teachers of what a good spirit message should consist of in terms of content. These methods are regularly successfully employed by many mediums and their spirit teams worldwide for the the communication of accurate spirit messages.

The CERT Formula

CERT was coined by noted Welsh medium and author Stephen O'Brien, who writes about it in his book *The Power of Your Spirit.* The CERT method is widely utilized as a structured approach in the United Kingdom for the delivery of spirit messages, both from the platform or in private sessions. Mediums trained in this method divide a typical message that they receive into four sections. As a formula, it is time-tested and highly effective as a means of conveying the information received by the medium to the recipient. The formula is divided into the following four parts, all of which have distinct relevance in terms of the content of the spirit message.

C Communicator

A communicator could be a loved one, friend or anyone in the spirit world that needs for, whatever purpose, to come through for the recipient of the message. Remember, spirit communicators may not always be the deceased loved one that the recipient wants or expects to hear from at the time.

E Evidence

Traditional Spiritualist mediums who use this approach attempt to further validate the identity of spirit communicators by providing as many evidential details about them as possible. This information is extensive and includes trivialities and details known only to the recipient.

R Reason

There are many reasons why a spirit may desire to come through. The CERT formula places emphasis on providing evidence through establishing solid recognition of the communicator with the recipient. It does not take into account that sometimes the message or reasons for the spirit coming through are more important than the identity of the communicator. Spirit communicators are not always motivated solely by the desire to provide survival evidence. They may strongly desire to impart healing or guidance for the recipient in regards to his or her material situation. In many cases, the reasons for the communication may be intended for the healing and soul progression of the spirit and less so than for the recipient of the message.

T Tie it Up

The conclusion of every spirit communication should formally bring together the above elements of the message with a final message from the spirit communicator. The traditional Spiritualist approach to mediumship as found in this formula demands that information about the communicating spirit be accepted by the recipient. Obtaining recognition from the recipient of the spirit personalities identity is the focus of traditional Spiritualist mediumship. In the UK, many mediums spend considerable time bringing through countless, evidential facts that must be understood. If the information is vague or not recognized, such mediums will ask for more from the spirit communicators, until the recipient is able to satisfactorily identify the spirits coming through.

Mediums working with this formula will attempt to provide the following information in every communication that they deliver in public demonstrations or private sessions. Although the order of the following information may vary among mediums, once an organized structure for presenting evidence is established with their spirit team, the details will be given in the same way for pretty much every communication.

- **Name**
- **Address:** (Physical locations associated with the communicator.)
- **Relationship**
- **Age**
- **Physical Description**
- **Character Description**
- **Personality**
- **Health Conditions**
- **Manner and Conditions of Passing**
- **Hobbies**
- **Physical Objects:** (Within the family or associated with the communicator.)
- **Shared Memories**
- **Knowledge of Recent Events:** Details about a family illness or the recipient having to change a flat tire on a busy motorway establishes the fact that the spirits are actively observing what is taking place in our physical lives.
- **Unknown Information:** The delivery of information that is completely unknown to the recipient at the time of delivery by the medium is known as a Test Message as it is always information that may be validated at a later date. Such a message proves beyond doubt that the personality survives physical death.

Simply put, the CERT formula has a beginning, middle and end. With structured mediumship this same system may be applied regardless of whether it is a public demonstration or private session.

Create Your Own Personal Formula

Another structured approach for receiving evidential communications developed by British medium Norman Hutt and described in his book *Searching for Spirit* is the NORM formula, which involves receiving four pieces of information relating to the spirit communicator. Name, Occupation, Residence and Manner of Passing: "I have an older man named John, who worked as a banker, lived in Manhattan and passed over due to heart failure."

My Own Approach

My format for delivering spirit communication varies depending on the circumstances and needs of the recipient. Generally, I will start out with one communicator, who often will assist others in coming through. The qualities of the spirit emphasized in the communication are either positive attributes needed by the recipient or unhealthy patterns possessed by the recipient that need to be overcome. I focus primarily on the strongest spirit communicator as this results in a more substantial and evidential message. The longer a medium is able to substain a mental link the better.

In some of the mediumship training programs that I facilitate, I instruct my students to isolate individual phases of mediumship with specific pieces of information be brought through in exact order. For example, I present an exercise for the students to work only with their clairaudience to receive the following details: the name of the communicator, music or a song, a phrase or sentence and the name of a physical location: "I am hearing the name of *Martha*, the song; '*You are my Sun-*

shine', the words; '*I am with you always'* and I am hearing her say; 'I lived in Boston.'"(See Exercise 39.)

I require students to receive spirit messages utilizing only one phase of mediumship with specific content. This disciplines their mediumship by forcing them to conform to an organized system. This requirement is not limited and may be applied successfully with any phase of mediumship: clairvoyance, clairaudience, clairsentience, etc. I suggest students of mediumship devise a personal formula for structure and insist the spirit helpers comply when transmitting communications.

Mitzie Monroe Method

The late Mitzie Monroe was a Spiritualist minister and medium who pastored a church in California for many years. She instructed her students in this basic formula for obtaining recognizable evidence from communicating spirit personalities. The Reverend Alfred Connor, who studied with her for many years, told me about this format and recommended that I try it out. I have served her former church and know mediums trained directly by her or indirectly by her students. As a result of this uniform training, they all present their mediumship in the same manner.

When the spirit presents themselves to the medium, they lightly touch the side of the medium to indicate, which side of the recipients family are they from. Left side for the father's and the right side for the mother's. The location of where they touch also enables the medium to know the height of the communicating spirit, which in this approach should be measured by head size and not feet and inches or centimeters, etc: "I have an older gentleman coming in from spirit, who is one head taller than me." Measuring in head sizes makes it easier for the recipient to understand the height of the spirit coming through.

The communicating spirit's gender, build, conditions of passing and relationship to the recipient should also be presented along with a description of what he or she is wearing and other details about his or her life. The spirit may be holding an object relating to his or her former physical life or an item as gift with significance for the recipient. The message or reason for coming through will also be presented. This method has a distinct beginning, middle and end which is short and to the point. Although sufficient information to validate the identity of the spirit communicator is provided, the format leaves room for equal or greater emphasis on the personal guidance or suggestions being conveyed for the recipient.

Family Tree Method

The medium envisions a tree trunk with many branches overlaying the physical body and position of the recipient in front of them. The communicating spirit personalities will present themselves in various positions branching out from the recipient based on their relationship to the recipient and the side of the family they are from.

- Left side is father
- Right side is mother
- To the side of mother and father indicates uncles and aunts
- In front of the sitter and below indicates a child or younger generation.
- Above the parents indicates grandparents on that side of the family
- To the side of grandparents indicates great-uncles and aunts
- Branch above grandparents indicates great-grandparents
- To the side indicates great-great-uncles and aunts
- An infant may be held in the hands of his or her parents or another significant relative from his or her generation.
- The parents or closest relatives may also place their hands upon the shoulders of the recipient. Such contact indicates the intimacy of the relationship.

The above structured formulas are presented as proven methods for the receiving and delivery of quality, reliable messages from the spirit world. I suggest that the students of mediumship attempt to utilize elements of any of these formulas or variations in a manner that works best for their needs.

The most important thing to remember is that mediumship should never be robotic or a cookie cutter approach. Each medium is an unique instrument and as such the approach to mediumship should be individualistic. One weakness of the CERT or any other structured approach is that mediums working in this manner may end up becoming too rigid in their presentation and unable to work outside the formula should information be presented differently.

Linking In Exercises

EXERCISE 62

Envelope Linking In

Teacher has participants write random marks on paper which is sealed in an envelope, numbered for identification, selected by another participant from a container and taken home. The participants are instructed to meditate outside of class holding the envelope for the purpose of mentally linking with spirit communicators connected with the owner of the envelope. Whatever information is obtained is written down and brought in to be shared with the group. Emphasis should be upon receiving specific, evidential facts that may be validated by the recipient. After sharing with the rest of the group what they have received, feedback may be given by the recipients.

EXERCISE 63

Names Linking In

The teacher gives participants the names of three individuals connected closely connected with them. The people may be physically living or deceased. Participants tune in outside of the group to the spirit world and attempt to determine if the names are of people who are still physically present or who have passed over, as well as details about them. The information is written down and brought into class and shared. The teacher may provide feedback about the individuals named in the assignment and the results of the members of the group.

CHAPTER 12

Public Demonstrations

A group mediumship session, large or small, differs from an individual mediumship session because more unique energies must blend to create the conditions for communication. Mediumship requires cooperation between the team of spirit helpers, the medium and the recipients. Unfortunately, recipients of mediumship in both individual sessions and larger demonstrations, do not always provide the energy necessary for favorable results. Disharmonious vibrations brought into a mediumship session weaken the delicate energetic and telepathic connections established by the spirit operators.

Individuals attend a demonstration of mediumship with a list of expectations of which spirit loved ones they want to receive communications from and what guidance they want to hear. A good medium, despite unfavorable circumstances, needs to learn how to handle working with such situations and raise the vibrations to obtain satisfactory results. There are several types of group sessions that practicing mediums may encounter, each needing to be handled differently.

The Message Circle/Seance

The message circle or seance involves the medium bringing through personal spirit messages for everyone present. There could be twenty-five or more people in such a circle, although the energy in smaller groups is generally easier to work with. A message circle could take place at a private residence, a Spiritualist church, a rented hall, or another site.

A message circle done in the confines of a personal residence in most cases is extremely powerful, as such gatherings usually are composed of family and close friends. The psychic atmosphere within a private residence is also typically more harmonious compared to a rented hall or space used for other activities. Messages circles may be challenging or easy for individual mediums. It all depends on who is attending and why.

Larger Demonstrations

Public demonstrations take on a whole different dynamic than platform mediumship done within the harmonious environment of a Spiritualist church or a smaller message circle. A public demonstration may be held in a theater, a rented hall, or auditorium. The audience at such venues usually is not as sympathetic or cordial as those in attendance at a Spiritualist worship service. The audience may include skeptics, the curious and the bereaved seeking communications from specific loved ones. Often, the emphasis at a larger demonstration will be on reaching a shorter number of recipients with longer, more evidential messages from recognizable spirit communicators.

Spiritualist Worship Services or Meetings

The congregation at a Spiritualist worship service understand the process of spirit communication and contribute sympathetic, positive energy to the medium. At some Spiritualist churches the medium is expected to reach as many recipients as possible with shorter spirit greetings. In other churches platform mediums are expected to provide longer, more detailed evidential communications.

Media Appearances

Radio and Television

Demonstrating mediumship on television or the radio is a wonderful opportunity to present mediumship to a wider audience of people, who know little or nothing about the subject. Mediums may also come across poorly in such situations, so it is crucial that each individual situation be carefully assessed by the medium prior to agreeing to work on the particular program. Some questions to ask are:

Is the program live or prerecorded? Both live or prerecorded have their advantages, but keep in mind that with prerecorded programs editing can take place, which may result in making a satisfactory demonstration of mediumship look horrible. Once the program is taped the medium will have little or no say in what is done with the content. Parts may be left out, inserted with other pieces, and in general edited in a way that may make the medium appear unfavorably. Mediums need to be especially careful as this can happen due to ignorance even with programs seemingly favorable to mediumship.

Live television and radio differs from prerecorded programming in that there is no editing involved and the medium must respond appropriately, when being interviewed or bringing through spirit communications. In both prerecorded and live programs, the medium must learn to work under pressure and on the spot.

What is the style of the host or interviewer on the program? Are they aggressive or confrontational? Do they believe in psychic phenomena or are they skeptical in a negative way? Have they featured psychics or mediums on their programs before and, if so, what was their approach?

What is the general viewing or listening audience of the program? Viewing or listening to previous shows, especially ones featuring interviews with other mediums provides an idea of what to expect. Remember that a confrontational or skeptical host is not necessarily a bad thing. What is important is whether the medium feels comfortable handling such a challenge and knowledgeable and sufficiently skilled as a medium to deal with an unsympathetic host or viewing audience.

If the focus of the program is lowbrow entertainment and the host likely to ridicule the medium or ask trivial or inappropriate questions, then the medium should politely refuse to participate. Sometimes programmers or hosts, who are antagonistic toward mediumship or think that the entire subject is complete delusion, may deliberately act as though they believe in it for the purpose of gaining the mediums trust in order to get them to appear on the program. Once the medium is in the controlled studio atmosphere the true colors of the host may unexpectedly be revealed and the trapped medium is forced to react to negative interrogation and ridicule.

It is, also, essential to know if any other guests are scheduled, and, if so, what is their disposition toward mediumship? Keep in mind that if the show is prerecorded, the medium's remarks or demonstration potentially could be edited between negative comments or unfavorable footage. Despite any strong desire for working on television or radio, mediums need to especially careful.

When appearing on television the medium should be appropriately attired and groomed. The medium needs to be aware that at all times, they are representing the spirit world and, as such, they must be careful in how they respond to questions as well as how they come across when delivering spirit messages.

A skilled host or others trained in debate and interviewing tactics can easily verbally demolish even a highly developed medium, if the medium is inexperienced or easily intimidated. Preparation is the key to coming across well in all respects. It would be good for mediums wanting to work on television or radio to practice responding to hostile questioning. Such an exercise may be recorded for the medium to view or listen to and access aspects of their presentation that may need improvement.

Television and radio appearances featuring mediumship may involve live call-ins or even bringing through communications for others in the studio possibly even a live studio audience. In general the psychic atmosphere of a radio station or television studio is not conducive for the process of spirit communication. The medium must bring their own energy to the meeting and establish a strong link with the spirit world regardless of the unfavorable vibrations and negativity from the host or others. Remember not all media hosts are negative. In most cases they are just ignorant about what mediumship is, and want the show to come across well. It is suggested, if possible, that mediums meet the host and others involved in the program, prior to the show to discuss what mediumship is and how it works.

The first time I worked in New Zealand as a medium in 1999, I appeared on regional and national radio and was the featured guest on the highly popular New Zealand television program *Good Morning*. The programmer and production team for the show, whom I met prior to the live broadcast, were all extremely supportive and made me feel at ease in the studio. Yet, the skeptical and high-strung host, Mary Lambie, was another story. Despite her attempts to verbally attack me and make me look bad, I was able to hold my own and bring through accurate spirit messages for live phone call-in's as well the manager of a Polynesian band that played live on that particular episode.

Platform Work

Mediums can only control their own energy, they have no control over other people or the psychic atmosphere present at the physical location of where they are working. As such mediums must pray and meditate as much as possible before hand and bring as high vibrations possible to the meeting. It is also important that mediums relax as much as possible in the hours prior to the demonstration as mental stress of any sort will affect their nervous system.

What is happening in the spirit world behind the scenes at such a public demonstration of medumship? The higher guides make arrangements, weeks before the scheduled meeting, preparing potential communicators connected to those physically planning on attending the meeting. The physical recipients of spirit messages are also influenced by the higher guides to attend the meeting. A few hours before the demonstration spirit loved ones connected to those physically attending the meeting are already waiting. Both the spirit communicator and message content in such a situation is carefully regulated by the higher guides. Potential communicators have trained and rehearsed their messages thoroughly with the skilled helpers of the medium and other specialists in the spirit world. The helpers of the medium function as intermediaries for the spirits coming through.

Other spirits congregate at the meeting to learn spiritual lessons and the mechanics of the process should they attempt at a later date to come through other mediums. There are also specialists in etheric chemistry who harmonize and build up the energy in preparation for the meeting. Mediums are able to control the vibrations and conditions of the proceedings if they are prepared. The vibrations at larger meetings are mixed and not always harmonious. What are some methods for mediums to raise the vibrations in such a situation?

A sense of humor always helps. Not everyone is a stand up comedian and when it comes to demonstrating mediumship there should always be reverence for the sacredness of communion with the spirit world. But reverence does not mean that mediums should be rigid. The spirit personalities retain their senses of humor after physical death and often make jokes when coming through. Platform mediumship requires good public speaking skills, and the ability to not take oneself too seriously. Joking helps to raise the energy and lighten up the proceeding by making the audience feel at ease.

Music and singing aids the harmony of meetings considerably and greatly assists in raising the vibrations. Songs do not need to be religious or spiritual in nature. What matters most is that the songs are well known by the participants. *You are my Sun Shine* or *I've been Working on the Railroad,* if sung with liveliness and enthusiasm, will do more to increase the psychic energy present than the lip-syncing of a religious hymn that resembles a funeral song. At Spiritualist meetings, I always prefer that *Battle Hymn of the Republic* or a similar upbeat number be sung, as the more fast-paced and uplifting the singing, the better.

When demonstrating mediumship, all the attention and the entire focus of everyone present is upon the medium. The medium must have mastered the art of closely working with the spirit world and be highly disciplined and in control of his or her spirit band. The more the medium is in control of the vibrations, the more he or she will be in control of the conditions. Besides superior presentation skills, the medium must know how to establish a favorable rapport with the audience and keep them involved throughout the demonstration. Audiences must be won over immediately in the first five minutes of the demonstration. If the audience feels left out they will soon get bored and lose interest resulting in the lowering of the vibrations present. There is one thing worse than an audience more dead than people in the spirit world and that is a medium who comes across as unenthusiastic and lifeless.

Being able to project the voice is essential as mediums need to not rely too much on technological advances such as microphones as in some cases they might not be available. When practicing delivery of spirit messages in the development circle, student mediums should get in the habit of projecting their voices and speaking as though they are standing in front of *50 or more* people. This method, although scary for those who are shy, nevertheless helps to train students properly in presentation and delivery of mediumship. Increasing the volume of the voice also enables the messages to come through stronger. Speaking softly from the platform should be avoided at all times for without a microphone the connection will be weaker and many will be unable to hear what is being said.

I remember seeing the late Alice Hughes, a noted Spiritualist medium from Albany New York, deliver at the age of 101, a spiritual address and spirit messages at a Spiritualist church service, without the assistance of a microphone. It was amazing listening as Hughes entire personality and disposition changed as her voice loudly boomed throughout the church. As she spoke, I clairvoyantly observed the faces of her spirit teachers overshadowing her features. Despite her advanced age, Hughes decorum and presentation skills were superb.

Platform mediums must learn to work with the voice vibration of the recipient and always ask permission before delivering a spirit message. A verbal response from the recipient energetically strengthens the connection and results in a smoother flow of information from the spirit world. Also, some people, despite being present, may not want for whatever reason to receive the communication.

In the USA, where I was trained in mediumship, I was taught that other than asking if the recipient understands the content of the message that mediums should refrain from asking unnecessary questions. Over the years, I have heard many mediums give the impression that they are fishing for information by asking questions such as: "Does anyone know someone in the spirit world who had the letter *J* in their name? Could it be a *John*, or a *James*?" This is why it is best for mediums to word information as a statement instead of a question: "I have a lady here who feels like a mother," instead of the classic, "Is your mother in spirit?"

A medium should ask recipients for confirmation without them volunteering information. This helps maintain the link between the medium, the communicating spirits, and the recipient. Also, by eliciting response from recipients of spirit messages, everyone watching the demonstration is involved and as a result is less likely to feel bored or get up and leave.

I used to give my students copies of articles written by skeptics critiquing the presentations of famous television mediums. Generally, the authors of such articles would point out the many unnecessary questions such mediums would ask as they believed that the mediums were cold reading the recipients. Ultimately, the less the medium knows the better. In situations where the content of the message is not understood the medium should ask the spirits for clarification or additional information. Mediums who strongly state what they receive project an impression of confidence in their abilities and trust in the accuracy of the information conveyed to them from the spirit world.

The Differences Between Mediumship in the USA and UK

The American approach to platform mediumship, when done correctly, tends to be straightforward and to the point. In the UK the approach to mediumship differs greatly from the American approach in terms of presentation style, as I learned the first time I observed a husband and wife team work as guest mediums at the Church of Two Worlds in Washington, DC.

The British wife had trained her American husband to world to work like her. I was surprised to see that instead of directly going to the recipient with a spirit message, they would indirectly receive the information about the spirit communicators and throw it out to the congregation in hopes that someone would be able to recognize it. At times, they would feel the spirit communicator needed to connect with someone located in a certain section of the pews. Often, many hands would be go up from people in the congregation, who could identify or place the information. When this happened they would attempt to bring through more pieces of evidential information, until finally only one individual could claim the contact.

After finding the correct recipient, it was mandatory for them to ask for four pieces of information that the recipient could understand as they wanted to make sure they were with the right person. They explained how important it was for them to make sure they were not psychically reading the aura of the recipient, but instead establishing a genuine link with the spirit world. Unlike American mediums, they would phrase the information they were receiving as questions and not direct statements. One man in congregation was asked if he liked or did art, a detail that did not make sense to the recipient. Finally, after many minutes of going back and forth, the man revealed he was a cook. "Well that's artistic," replied the medium.

The Aura or Spirit?

The idea behind presenting mediumship in this manner is the concern that an energetic pull toward someone sitting in the congregation is not necessarily a link with the spirit world. A medium could easily feel attracted to an individual wearing a bright, colorful shirt, or someone deliberately trying to mentally influence the medium to pick him or her for a message. In such cases, the medium is reading the aura of the recipient instead of obtaining genuine messages from the spirit world.

Many of the prominent British mediums I know hold such views and work indirectly asking many questions. Many are very uptight about making sure they are not reading the aura. According to them, the purpose of mediumship is to provide evidence of life after physical death and that messages containing guidance are psychic and not mediumistic. On the other hand, many mediums are directed by their helpers to the recipient and deliver solid mediumistic communications. It is important to emphasize that an energetic pull toward the recipient is not necessarily a psychic link. There is not one correct way to work with mediumship.

Information received mediumistically is not always purely evidential details about the spirit communicator. Often, the higher guides provide spiritual guidance to help the recipient. This is different from information obtained through reading the aura. Many UK mediums also feel that only evidential messages should be given in public demonstrations and that personal guidance should be saved for private consultations.

The spirit world decides the content of a communication and what the recipient needs to hear. While evidence at times is essential, spiritual guidance is not mundane information, but advice and suggestions from the wiser, loving perspective of higher guides in the spirit world. Spiritual growth and personal development matter the most. The purpose of mediumship is to touch the recipient on a soul level and help them to connect with God.

The Indirect Approach

The indirect approach of delivering evidential communications is largely archaic and unnecessary. It originates from the years when predicting the future was a criminal offense in the UK and Spiritualist mediums, to distinguish themselves from fortune-tellers, would focus on delivering purely evidential communications. In the older days of the Spiritualist movement public demonstrations were held in which the indirect approach functioned well as a means of presentation. In large, poorly lit halls, the medium could not always see everyone present and as a result the indirect approach was ideal.

Platform mediumship in the UK tends to emphasis evidence of survival, whereas in the USA more importance is placed on the message. The UK approach to platform mediumship involves longer time spent with the recipient compared to the USA approach of delivering shorter spirit messages or greetings. *Give a greeting, not a reading* is an old American Spiritualist maxim meant to prevent long-winded mediums from bringing through lengthy spirit messages at a public meeting for only a few and boring the rest of those in attendance.

A well-known international Scottish medium stated that in America the clairvoyant message work is *quantity over quality.* Another noted British medium condescendingly remarked, while teaching mediumship at an American Spiritualist community that all the resident mediums there were *a bunch of psychics.* In both cases, they were probably right.

In the USA there are many mediums who love the emphasis on detailed evidence demonstrated by leading UK Mediums. Many UK mediums work in the USA because they are paid well and their quality work is truly appreciated. I have demonstrated mediumship in the UK many times in most cases delivering shorter spirit greetings to as many people in the audience as possible. As a whole I received favorable feedback from UK audiences who shared that they found the typical indirect approach of delivering lengthy communications boring. The way mediumship is practiced in different countries has much to do with cultural differences, which influence the particular aspects of mediumship emphasized.

The Do's and Don'ts of Platform Work

When presenting mediumship in public mediums should be formally attired and well-groomed. After being introduced the medium should stand before those in attendance and allow his or her helpers in spirit to direct him or her to where the spirit messages are most needed.

It is good for mediums to start a demonstration by bringing through a communicator to someone seated in the back of the premises rather than just going to people seated toward the front. Doing this establishes a connection energetically with the entire space and makes it easier for communications to come through. As previously noted, mediums should always ask permission to come to the recipients of the communications and never ask questions. At the end of each message that is given, it is appropriate for mediums to conclude by saying: "I will leave you with that and say God bless you" or something similar to let the recipient know that they are finished.

How to Handle Problems

What are some of the potential problems that mediums might face when doing platform mediumship and what are the best approaches to dealing with them? Crying children, people talking, or noise from outside can potentially disturb demonstrating mediums by making them lose focus and break their link with the spirit world. A medium needs to discipline his or her mind to be able to mentally detach and completely block out all external noises or other distractions. People should always be told to turn off their cell phones and asked to be quiet should they be noisy, but in some situations these distractions cannot be avoided. It is up mediums to be in control of themselves and their mediumship at all times.

Inexperienced mediums may also find themselves losing their connection, if they allow the body language or responses of the recipient affect them. If the recipient doe not understand the information, the medium needs to go back to the spirit world and ask for more information to clarify what has been given. Generally this approach will result in additional pieces of information being provided by the spirit operators or things being worded in a different way so that the recipient understands.

Should the recipient be unable to place the information the medium needs to intuitively know when to move on to another recipient instead of beating a dead horse and dragging things out longer than necessary. Knowing when to quit is important as once the audience loses interest and the energy goes down, it will be very difficult to build up again. The medium might suggest to recipients that they take information with them and look into it or even to see them after the demonstration is finished so that more time may be spent but not at the expense of the meeting.

It is common for many spirit messages to be dismissed at the time they are received, due to recipients not recognizing the identities of the spirit communicators or not understanding the information conveyed. Yet, in many cases, either events develop as described by the medium, or the identities of of the unrecognized spirits, are remembered. Often, such identification takes places through the input of older relatives or others who validate facts about the spirit that the recipient was unaware of at the time of receiving the message. Examples such as this constitute some of the best evidence of survival as both the medium and the recipient knew absolutely nothing about the details conveyed. Mediums, regardless of whether doing a private session with an individual or delivering spirit messages to an audience of thousands of people, must trust the spirit world one-hundred-percent regardless of whether the spirit communications brought through by them are understood by the recipients.

Openly antagonistic or negatively disposed people in the audience also need to be handled properly by the medium. It is better to avoid working with such disharmonious individuals. Hecklers and psychologically disturbed individuals should to be asked to leave and escorted out of the premises by others who are present. Again, the mediums best defense is a solid connection with the spirit personalities and a disciplined mind that regardless of circumstances remains undisturbed and detached from the external surroundings.

People getting up and leaving the demonstration while the medium is working, besides being rude and showing a lack of reverence for what is taking place, may also disturb the psychic atmosphere or contribute to an undisciplined medium losing his or her focus. Sometimes people will even walk between the medium and the recipient of the communication. Mediums need to realize that such disturbances will happen occasionally, and regardless of the situation, should not affect their connection with the spirit world.

Discipline is the Key

A disciplined medium will be able to hold a link with one or more spirit communicators and go back and forth between them relaying evidence. It is natural for some mediums to quickly deliver the information they receive. Sometimes, inexperienced mediums will not want to pause or break this flow as they fear they will lose the connection. A skilled medium is able to hold a link with a spirit for a long period, even physically leave the room to return and instantly re-establish the connection.

Mediums should also learn how to double link with other mediums or even multiple mediums for obtaining information from the same spirit communicator. Many mediumistic artists doing spirit portraiture from the platform team with another medium to double link with the same communicating spirit. The psychic atmosphere created by the physical space also certainly affects the conditions in a favorable or unfavorable manner. Mediums need to learn that they can work anywhere with the spirit world and have an extremely powerful connection.

Sensitive and Negative Messages

Not all information given by mediums is what the recipient wants to receive. Generally, information given by the spirit operators within the context of a public demonstration should be conveyed regardless of what the medium thinks in terms of the appropriateness of the message. Higher guides never give information that cause embarrassment or emotional distress. Criticism about the recipient and information of a sensitive nature is always presented to the medium in a positive, constructive way. Obviously, for legal reasons, a medium should not attempt to medically diagnosis or prescribe from the platform, but the higher guides regulate each individual message and information received should be given out.

Many mediums may feel uncomfortable about delivering sensitive information in a public setting from the platform. But it is the responsibility of mediums to give a message exactly as they receive it and not change the content based on assumptions that it may embarrass or upset the recipient. The spirit helpers let mediums know when not to convey particular messages and instruct mediums to tell the recipient to meet with them privately at the conclusion of the demonstration. If the spirit father of a recipient comes through and says, "I was a total drunk," the medium should deliver the message as it has been given and not tone down the content by saying: "Your father liked a few." Such a message would not be permitted by the spirit controls, if it were to cause embarrassment or disturb the recipient. Swear words or inappropriate language are highly evidential in some cases and are often permitted to be conveyed during a private session, but not during a public demonstration. Unless the spirit helpers say otherwise, mediums should deliver the message as they receive it.

Once I gave a message to an elderly couple to exercise caution when opening a closet in their residence as heavy items stored on the upper shelves were unstable and could cause injury. An untrained medium may not understand how to properly interpret and deliver such a message. While warnings might be given in order to prevent a mishap, telling the recipient negative information such as he or she is going to die next week or be involved in a serious accident, generally would not come through with controlled, regulated mediumship. Negative messages generally have to do with the mediums lack of training and experience.

Assorted Mediumship Exercises

EXERCISE 64

Pretending To Be A Medium

This is a variation of an exercise shared by the late Dan Duffy, an outstanding medium from Massachusetts, who introduced it to my open development class as a guest instructor one week while I was away. Participant stands up in front of the group and pretends to be a medium by delivering fake spirit messages for the others in the group. The participant is told not to genuinely bring through spirit messages, but to move and speak like a medium and make up nonsense communications. The teacher will prompt the participant with suggestions or questions relating to information, he or she should pretend to receive. The participant should spontaneously make stuff up about the fictitious spirit personalities that he or she are pretending to bring through. Emphasis should be on making up evidential details about fake spirit people.

After the participant has worked with at least several members of the group bringing through fake messages, the teacher should ask if any of the information for each individual made sense to the recipients of the messages. If this exercise is done correctly, with the right prompting from the teacher, the participant, instead of making the information up, will actually start to bring through recognizable information from the spirit world. This should be a fun exercise and done in the spirit of having a good time.

This exercise is not meant to trivialize mediumship or encourage dishonesty. Mediums should never make things up or pretend to bring through spirits. The purpose of this exercise is to assist students to get their analytical minds out-of-the-way and channel evidential information from the spirit world. Although it may feel that they are making up things, students will notice a shift take place energetically as the information conveyed shifts from made up messages to genuine spirit communications. The others in the group should observe the subtle shift as the connection changes from the imagination to receiving information transmitted from the spirit world. At the conclusion of this exercise recipients of the phony messages may provide feedback about any information given that has made sense.

EXERCISE 65

Platform Indirect

Participant stands up in front of group and first receives evidential impressions about a spirit communicator, not knowing who the recipient is to be. After relating sufficient evidence, the participant asks spirit helpers to direct him or her to a recipient, who should be able to confirm that he or she can identify the details given. Feedback may be given by recipients.

EXERCISE 66

Indirect With Questions

Participant stands up in front of group. Teacher prompts participant by asking questions in order to facilitate the receiving of additional information. Questions regarding both general and specific details may be asked as such as the gender of the communicator or the exact month and date of his or her birth, etc.

EXERCISE 67

One Ahead With Cards

Instructor places a deck of inspirational cards in front of participants seated in circle. Participants takes turns picking a card and linking into the spirit world to indirectly bring through recognizable spirit personalities along with messages for an unknown recipient. Participants are told to pay attention to each message. Once everyone works the instructor reveals that the recipient of each communication is for the individual seated to the left of the medium.

CHAPTER 13

Private Sessions

Divine Spirit, God. Surround us with your love, light and healing. I ask that I be used as an instrument to bring through information and guidance to help with the practical as well as the spiritual. I ask that the highest and the best of angel loved ones and guides work with me and through me and I ask, God, that I be used as a clear and accurate instrument for this communication. May the words of my mouth and the meditations of my heart be acceptable in your sight. Infinite Spirit, my strength and inspiration. Amen.

A private mediumship session may be a great challenge or a blessing of considerable proportion. The success or failure of a session ultimately depends upon the energy or psychic conditions that are present at the time of the session. There are no clear-cut rules on how to conduct a mediumship session, but there are some pointers and general guidelines which will help bring about the best possible results for recipient of the communications as well as the medium. In the UK, the term *sitting* is widely used by mediums as it distinguishes a mediumship session from a psychic reading. In other places, the term *reading* is used to describe a mediumship session, as well as a host of other types of intuitive readings from Tarot cards to astrology. As a medium, I have never liked either of these terms and prefer the term *session*.

Psychic Readings

A mediumship session differs from a psychic or fortune-telling type of reading. While the process is similar in that both involve the utilization of intuitive ability, the approach and results differ drastically. In a psychic reading the sensitive will use his or her intuitive ability to establish a telepathic link with the energy field of the person he or she is working with or the psychic vibrations present within an object or a physical space. In some cases, cards may be used and systems such as numerology and astrology may be employed.

The energy involved in such a session feels different compared to the energy experienced when receiving mental impressions from personalities in the spirit world. With a psychic reading the vibrations experienced by the intuitive reader are on a mundane, denser level compared to the uplifting, invigorating energy involved in a mediumistic session.

Mediumship Sessions

Mediumship involves establishing a telepathic connection with personalities residing the spirit world. The rate of vibration in the spirit world is much quicker than the frequency of vibration in the physical world and as such the spirits must lower their energy to mentally link with the medium. In order to establish the strongest possible connection, the medium, through meditation and prayer, must raise his or her own vibrations as much as possible and meet the spirits at least halfway, if not more. This is true for both private sessions and mediumship demonstrations involving larger numbers of people.

Regardless of how many people are present, the successful medium must learn to work with less-than-ideal energy and manage his or her own vibration throughout the session or demonstration. With a private mediumship session the recipient may or may not bring the right conditions necessary for achieving the best results.

Enthusiasm Necessary

The energy that someone brings to a session may greatly enhance or hinder the communications that take place. Love, harmony and enthusiasm build the psychic power and make conditions ideal for the spirit world to come through. Negative skepticism, intense anxiety, anger or depression and general lack of enthusiasm create a mental atmosphere, which is counterproductive for transmitting and receiving spirit messages. If the recipient is lethargic and sits facing the medium as dead as a corpse, then the results naturally will be affected. I encounter many recipients who are difficult to work with for a variety of reasons. Sometimes with such individuals or groups, the energy is so low and the chemistry so disharmonious that I feel as though there is literally a wall between myself and those sitting in front of me.

I find that it is always helpful when the recipient is knowledgeable about the mechanics of the process, or at least sympathetically disposed. Being antagonistic or wanting things done a certain way, without question, will almost always lead to unfavorable results. I have worked with many individuals over the years, who have come to me for mediumship sessions, but have been difficult and disharmonious to work with.

Without fail, and many times unintentionally, such recipients bring the wrong energy with them resulting in a session that falls far short of what it could be in all respects. When the conditions are satisfactory, the energy is high and the information effortlessly flows as it is conveyed from the spirits to the medium, who articulates it to the recipient. I have experienced many difficult sessions, in which I felt as though I mentally had to pull the information from the spirit world.

In most cases, an individual coming for a session wants contact with the spirit world; otherwise he or she would not have made the appointment. Occasionally, individuals reluctantly may schedule a private session with a medium because someone else forced them into it, or got them to go, without telling them what they were getting into. In the majority of cases, the person coming for the session wants to hear what the medium has to say and despite not understanding the process is receptive to the information that comes through. The problem that arises is that some people are uneducated about the mechanics of the process and arrive at the session with a preconceived idea of what should happen, as well as an agenda of what they want to hear, and who they want to talk to in the spirit world.

Television shows and Hollywood films give people the wrong ideas about mediumship. The heavily edited, episodes of television programs featuring mediums, also create the false conception that every session with a medium results in instant communication with anyone in the spirit world the recipient wants to contact. Nothing could be further from the truth as no medium can call up particular spirit personalities and, often, those coming through for a variety of reasons are not instantly identified or even known by the recipient.

Reasons Mediums are Consulted

What are some of the reasons that people seek to have sessions with a medium? The physical death of a loved one or someone dear to the recipient may create a strong desire to establish contact with the spirit world through a medium. The closure and healing that may be achieved through a session is immense as is the resulting firm conviction, after receiving evidential communications through a medium that life survives the destruction of the physical body.

Skeptics may also seek the services of mediums, not necessarily to debunk what they consider delusional or fraudulent, but, often, because they are curious and want to see for themselves if it is possible to communicate with the dead. Such skeptics when convinced by the evidence presented through mediums find their perspective of reality altered completely and their consciousness transformed spiritually as a result of the session.

Others seek the advice of the medium because they want to grow spiritually and improve themselves on a soul level. Such people are less concerned about hearing from deceased loved ones. They accept the reality of life after physical death and are actively working on their soul-growth. I love working with people oriented this way, as they tend to be more on my wavelength, due to their personal interest in spirituality and higher consciousness.

Many people visit mediums not understanding anything about mediumship and how it differs from fortune-telling or mundane psychic readings. I commonly am asked inappropriate questions by such recipients such as: " I want to know if the man who I am having the affair with at work is going to leave his wife for me? I know that he's my soul mate because another psychic I went to told me that he was."

Generally, such individuals would be better served by consulting a Tarot card reader or psychic, who focuses on providing more materially oriented information. There is nothing wrong with fortune-telling as it is a stepping stone to mediumship. A psychic may tune in and pick up on extremely accurate pieces of information for a person such as: "You own a red car, but watch out one of the wheels is loose and will fall off," or "You are going to meet a man with a gold tooth, but watch out he's married."

While such information may be amazingly accurate and even entertaining, it does not help the recipient transform his or her consciousness and get closer to God. The individuals who seek fortune-telling are generally not on the same wavelength as a medium and want something completely different than spirit communication. Mediums need to accept that such recipients may never be satisfied with the results of the session, no matter how evidential.

Many individuals seek the services of mediums soon after the passing of a loved one and, too frequently, are left disappointed, when the particular loved one fails to come through. While the desired spirit party may communicate, no medium can guarantee contact from a specific spirit personality. A medium is only the instrument for the higher teachers and guides to work through.

How to Prepare for the Best Possible Results

When seeking a medium people ideally need to be in a balanced and healthy state of mind. Rushing from one medium to another in hopes of hearing from specific spirit people is not good. It is better for people to investigate mediumship in a sensitive and intelligent manner accepting that which makes sense and rejecting anything lacking such qualities.

It is always wise to pray and meditate before the session and ask for specific spirit personalities, if desired, to appear or for particular issues or problems to be addressed. The spirit guardians, who orchestrate the session, know the overall situation in people's lives and do their best to bring through what is needed at the given time. It may not be what a person wants to hear, but it will be what the spirit guardians are able to come through with at the given time for the highest good and growth of the recipient.

A calm mind is conducive for receiving the best results. Intense emotions or wanting things done a certain way does the exact opposite by creating a dense psychic atmosphere that makes it harder for the communication to take place. Remember, mediumship is all about having harmonious conditions between the minds of the medium, recipient, and communicating spirit personalities. A successful session is achieved largely by all parties involved being on the same wavelength. When this is the case the telepathic ideas and information are not only effectively transmitted by the spirit operators, but they are accurately received and conveyed by the medium. Mediumship is all about team work and in order for the private session to go smoothly, the medium must trust his or her team of spirit helpers completely.

False Expectations

An appointment with a medium is also an appointment with the spirit world. There should be reverence for the process as well as respect for the medium and the communicating spirits. Unfortunately, many people lack proper reverence for the process and lack respect for the medium. They want the medium to do their bidding by answering their questions, solving their problems and bringing through everybody in the spirit world they wish to call up. If the medium is unable to live up to their expectations or satisfy their demands, however unreasonable, then the medium is blamed and labeled inadequate and possibly a fraud.

An enthusiastic, positive minded recipient is easiest to work with when doing mediumship as he or she helps to create, with his or her favorable mindset, a psychic atmosphere that blends with the energy field of the medium. The members of the medium's spirit team, who have lowered their rate of vibration to mentally and energetically connect with the medium, also find it easier to work with such individuals.

Mediumship can be compared to a cell or mobile phone in that when the connection is good the voice at the other end can be heard loudly and clearly. However, even the most expensive, technologically sophisticated cell phone will not function properly, if taken into the desert or the middle of nowhere. When there is little or no connection, the messages on a cell phone will be incomplete, garbled or nonexistent. People generally don't blame their cell phones when things go wrong, especially when the battery is not charged. But with mediumship recipients will blame the medium, little realizing that they are the fault that the results achieved are lacking. Intense anxiety, negativity or narrow-minded skepticism brought to a mediumship session create the wrong type of psychic atmosphere and lead to failure.

In chapter 12 the details of what takes place behind the scenes prior to a group session are explained. The same preparation on the part of the medium's spirit team and potential communicators applies to private sessions. The spirit guides of the recipient decide upon the content of the session and the spirits chosen to come through.

The quality of the information conveyed during a session is determined largely by the mentality and spirituality of the medium. It is wrong to criticize mediums based on the type of information they receive from the spirit world. Some mediums possess an aptitude for receiving certain types of messages from the spirit world. This does not mean they are superior in skill to other mediums, who in turn, due to their mental makeup, receive other types of information more efficiently.

The success of a mediumship session is incredibly subjective as recipients want different things. Some desire higher spiritual guidance, others seek evidence or messages from deceased loved ones, and many more want their fortunes told. Many mediums prefer to know what their clients want before they start the session. This way they are better able to focus on the needs of the client without spending valuable time concentrating on areas the client may not feel are not as important.

My Own Approach for Conducting a Session

I prefer not knowing anything about individuals I work with and I emphasis this when they initially schedule the session. What the recipient wants to hear or thinks they need is secondary to the information the higher spirit teachers know will most benefit the recipient. Many times, an individual comes to a session and wants to do all the talking, potentially volunteering all sorts of personal information, which as a medium, I do not want or need to hear. Often, I have to emphasis to people not to talk while I am working other than to acknowledge what I am getting with a simple, "Yes," when understood, or: "I don't understand. Could you give me a little more information for clarification please?" when unsure about the details being presented.

Whenever I am about to conduct a mediumship session for a client, I try to spend at least five minutes or more explaining what mediumship is, how I work as a medium and what to expect during a session. This introduction is important as it educates those coming for sessions who may not know, other than what they have seen on television, very little, if anything, about the process or what it entails. I find that the more educated someone is about the nature of mediumship, the easier the he or she will be to work with during a session.

After briefly explaining how it works and what to expect, I take the hands of my client and pray out loud asking for the highest and the best of those in the spirit world to bring through information and guidance to help the recipient with his or her soul-growth. At the close of the session, I also hold the recipient's hands and pray expressing gratitude to God. While some people may not feel comfortable with the religious nature of prayer, I feel that praying aloud at both the beginning and end of each session is important as it creates an atmosphere of reverence.

The act of holding hands is genuinely healing, warm and caring and helps establish trust between them and myself. It also helps me to energetically connect with them, which strengthens my connection with the spirits involved in the session. The recipient sitting across from me functions energetically as a battery by providing power for the session. When the power is high the messages come through clearly containing specific details. Should the power be flat or low the messages tend to more generalized and vague. Most people coming for a mediumship session are weak batteries. They have a particular agenda about what they want to hear and they could not care less about the process. This is not to fault them as they just do not know any better.

How to Handle Difficult Recipients

Clients coming to me for session may be extremely demanding and pushy in wanting to hear from particular spirits or seeking answers to specific issues. Many years ago a man showed up for a private session. Once I started the session, he would not let me bring through what the spirit world wanted to tell him, instead he proceeded to pull out a large note-book with questions written on every line for at least three or four pages. The whole session consisted of him reading the questions to see what my response would be. He even asked me what lottery numbers I got for him. Mediums need to be in control and not allow clients to intimidate them or manipulate the session.

Mediums should refuse to work with anyone who seems overly negative or psychologically disturbed. The mission of mediumship is to serve God and help others, yet it is important for practicing mediums to protect themselves energetically from negative or disharmonious people by declining to work with them. Most people who come to a medium feel entitled if they are paying money for a session to receive particular results. Although the process of mediumship is a science, it is not an exact science and as such every session is highly experimental with results never guaranteed.

The ability to share spiritual light and higher guidance from the spirit world as a medium is a privilege and a great blessing. On the other hand, each situation is different and it is important for practicing mediums to trust their intuition. Should a medium feel uncomfortable with working with a particular person, they should trust their intuition and, if possible, refer the individual to another medium or appropriate practitioner. In general, nobody should be turned away because of financial hardship, external appearance, or the prejudices of the medium.

What if the Recipient Does Not Favor the Content of the Session?

Obviously, it is important to be accurate as a medium, but the information that is conveyed during the session is determined by higher spirits. It is not the fault of the medium if someone does not like what has come through. Both praise and criticism from the recipient should be met with detachment. Mediums are responsible for being accurate instruments and giving out what they receive without adding details or leaving anything out. Sometimes, the psychic conditions present, combined with a lack of ability for the spirits to sufficiently communicate, hinder the process of communication.

However, a recipient may not understand how the process works or have unrealistic, preconceived expectations of what should take place. This mentality combined with possible anticipation, anxiety or even negative skepticism creates a disharmonious chemistry that detrimentally affects the results. It is important to note that with some recipients a medium could provide specific information about their deceased loved ones, including names and other factual information, and the recipient, due to inexperience, still would not recognize the information.

This is not to say that mediums are always right. The medium can easily make mistakes, but the tendency that I have observed over the years is that mediums generally are blamed for the content of the messages they receive that the recipients do not like or understand for whatever reasons. These individuals care only about having their trivial questions answered or hearing from specific spirit people. Such people are ignorant of the limitations of the process and that the higher spirit teachers set the agenda for the session not themselves.

Why Some Spirits Don't Come Through

Spirit personalities are not always ready to communicate. They may be occupied elsewhere and unavailable at the time of the session. They are not under anyone's *beck and call* and the greatest priority in their life is not always communication with loved ones through a medium. This is especially true of spirits, suffering from intense emotional trauma or imbalances, prefer to focus on healing themselves from whatever mental baggage or disharmonious conditions that they have brought with them into the spirit world.

As discussed in Chapter 12 the spirits also must learn the process, which requires instruction from qualified helpers in the spirit world, who specialize in guiding and training individuals to communicate through mediums with their loved ones and others in the physical world. This does not happen overnight, although there certainly are cases in which spirit loved ones, in their eagerness or desperation to make contact, will make an all-out effort to master the process, as quickly as possible, in order to come through a medium.

A Few Interesting Experiences

"I only want to hear from my high level guides and nobody else!" A woman loudly announced to me before I commencing the session. Not surprisingly, the main communicator was her aunt, an individual she did not get along with. While in the physical world the aunt was plagued with psychological problems that she was still trying to overcome while in the spirit world. The woman in turn possessed many of the same issues.

Such a session is also for the benefit of the communicating spirit personality. Many people do not realize that just because someone has passed over and is able to communicate through a medium that they are automatically on a higher, more evolved level. We take our problems and negative character defects with us. In the physical world we can cut corners and cheat others. We cannot cheat or get away from the consequences of our actions for in the spirit world, in order for progression to take place, retribution and amends must be made.

I remember at the close of my annual psychic mediumship retreat in Massachusetts, I did private sessions for several of the attendees. One of my students attending from upstate Vermont wanted a private session as it was an anniversary connected with a dearly departed relative. She had felt this spirit loved one around her the entire weekend and desperately wanted to make contact.

To her surprise, this relative did not communicate at all during the session. Instead, I described another spirit and related many details that she instantly recognized. The unexpected communicator had lived in her neighborhood during her childhood. She remembered him well as he had been a convicted child molester abusing many children in the community where she had grown up. She understood completely why he was coming through, as it related to particular situations that she was dealing with in her physical life.

During a mediumship session, major questions need not be asked as generally the answers are provided by the higher guides. Still, I like to give clients the opportunity to ask questions should they need further clarification about information that has come through or other concerns that have not been addressed. I find that toward the end of the session is a good time for questions. I would rather they ask me questions during the session than think of questions they forgot to ask while driving home.

People have all sorts of weird, sometimes inappropriate questions. An elderly woman in New Zealand wanted me to find out if her deceased husband had ever cheated on her as she had found evidence of a decades-old affair. The spirit husband did come through to ask for forgiveness and encouraged her with healing for other psychological issues that were affecting her in a negative way. Because of her anger toward him, due to her suspicions about his lack of fidelity, she was not receptive to any of his positive, loving input. Individuals do change when they go to the spirit world. It is not always instant, but the opportunity for personal progression and improvement is always there.

Tape Record the Session

In Toronto, Canada, I did a private session for a man who had consulted many mediums over the years. During the session a fatherly spirit came in the strongest. The man left the session satisfied as he had found the information provided of great value. He had not told me that he did recognize the fatherly spirit and as a result, even though he was happy with the session, he assumed that I had been totally wrong with what I had said. Upon arriving home, he played the tape recording of the session to his wife, who instantly recognized the spirit as being her deceased stepfather. Recipients should always be encouraged to tape the session as you never know what parts of the session will be relevant at a later date.

"I want to know when I am going to die? Can you tell me?" asked a man, who came to see me for a session in Virginia. My sense of humor kicked in, and I responded by stating, "Thursday at 4:30 PM. This week!" I had to explain to him that I was joking. Even if the higher spirits knew the time of our physical death, they would not share it with us.

Phone Sessions

Private sessions by phone or Skype function the same as in person sessions. Through some may question the value of a phone session, many mediums and recipients find them to be effective. Each situation is unique. Phone sessions can be fantastic or a complete failure. The session is a reciprocal relationship and the energy must be balanced by both parties to have the best possible connection.

A phone session, despite the physical distance, works the same as the recipient sitting across from the medium. During a phone session, we begin with a prayer, just as we would in person. The vocal response of recipients helps mediums better connect with their vibration, while linking in with the spirit world.

Mixed Energies

It is not uncommon for individuals to want another party such a spouse or close friend to sit in on the session as an observer and not as a participant. Everyone present at the session is participating as a battery. Unless the other parties contribute positive energy to the session, it better to restrict the session to the individual recipient. On the other hand, there is nothing like having a family or close group of friends come for a session as often the messages will be for all of the parties present. Sometimes spirit communicators, who are related to friends or acquaintances of the recipient, will come through with messages they want to pass on to the other party.

Infinite Spirit, we thank you for the love and guidance that has come through and for the opportunity to connect with each other as well as commune with our angel friends and loved ones. Please bless this child with your healing light and may he/she always be aware of your unconditional love and the higher inspiration and divine light that guides them. We thank you God for the sharing and blessing that has taken place. Amen.

Assorted Mediumship Exercises

EXERCISE 68

Make Believe Spirits

Participants sit in circle. Taking turns clockwise around the circle, each participant quickly makes up a phony spirit communicator emphasizing specific evidential information. For maximum effectiveness participants should take turns around the circle at least three times creating three fictitious spirits.

I have a spirit here named Richard, who served in as a Navy cook in the Vietnam war. When he didn't like an officer he deliberately put nuts, bolts and metal objects in the food so they would break their teeth. He was born on March 8 and loved to listen to Jimi Hendrix albums.

The objective of this exercise is for mediums to get the analytical mind out of the way and to spontaneously give out evidential details. The more the mind is programmed to receive specific evidence regarding spirit communicators, the more such detailed information will be conveyed. Obviously, honesty is essential for mediums, but for the sake of this exercise medium's should actively use their imaginations.

EXERCISE 69

Unknown Occupants of Chairs

A few hours before a public demonstration of mediumship, several empty seats are chosen from among the chairs where those in attendance will sit. The medium attempts to receive evidential information from spirits connected to the individuals, who will later occupy the empty seats. This information should be recorded and shared later with the recipients. This exercise teaches mediums to directly link with the spirit world and cultivate absolute trust in the evidence provided.

EXERCISE 70

Creating Fictitious Spirits

At various intervals during the day create fictitious spirits and ultra-specific evidence about them. This exercise programs the mind to receive unusual evidential information.

I have a girl named Jennifer who passed over from falling into an open manhole on January 14. She wore a yellow clown costume at the time of her passing and worked as a teller at a bank. She loved the four gold fish she kept as pets and tended to forget about watering her plants.

I have a man named Albert who loved to pose nude for life drawing classes. He was a Korean war veteran and owned a factory that manufactured flags. His hobbies were skydiving and baseball cards. He lived on 55 Foster Avenue.

EXERCISE 71

Spirit Vehicle and Residence

Participants pair up, hold each other's hands and connect with a spirit communicator. Evidential information is strictly limited to details about the former vehicle used for transportation by the spirit such as a car, bicycle, or motorcycle. Participants attempt to receive memories from the spirit about both the interior of the vehicle and its exterior description. Next, participants receive information from the same communicator about his or her former physical residence. Describe as many details as possible about both the interior and exterior of the building.

EXERCISE 72

Past Memories

Participants pair up, hold each others hands and connect with the spirit world. Information is strictly limited to the memory of a specific incident relating to the former physical life of a spirit communicator.

I am receiving a memory about the time the striped cat ran up the Christmas tree knocking it over and breaking all the ornaments.

I am being shown the memory of a boy who fell through thin ice on a lake and was saved by a priest.

EXERCISE 73

Awareness of Present

Participants pair up, hold each others hands and link with the spirit world. Information is strictly limited to details about a recent incident involving the recipient. This exercise demonstrates that the spirits are around us and aware of what is taking place in our physical lives.

Last week you fell off the bed trying to reach your socks on the floor.

You had a flat tire last Thursday. A man with a beard in a blue truck stopped and helped you change it.

EXERCISE 74

Physical Objects

Participants pair up, hold each others hands and link with the spirit world. Information is strictly limited to a description of a physical object associated with a spirit that is still materially present. Pieces of jewelry, photographs, and other easily validated heirlooms are highly evidential to convey. Participants can proceed with further details about the spirit communicator.

Chapter 14

Spiritual Healing

Prayer for Spiritual Healing
I ask the Great Unseen Healing Force
to remove all obstructions from my mind and body
and to restore me to perfect health.
I ask this in all sincerity and honesty
and I will do my part.

I ask this Great Unseen Healing Force
to help both present and absent ones
who are in need of help
and to restore them to perfect health.
I put my trust in the love and power of God.

Spiritual healing is the most important gift from spirit and the phase of mediumship most needed in this modern age. Historically, in all cultures there have been individuals who functioned as healers and intermediaries for the spirit personalities to work through. While culturally the approach to healing may vary with the physical techniques or rituals employed, the essence of the healer attuning to a higher spiritual power for the purpose of healing remains the same.

Jesus was known for laying on of hands. As with many forms of spiritual healing, hands are a focal point for directing the healing energies. The hands of the healer also represent the intention of the healer to alleviate suffering. As a form of mediumship, spiritual healing is both a mental phase and a physical phase. It is a mental phase because the intuitive mind of the healer must be in attunement with the healing source. It is a physical phase because through healing mediumship direct physiological changes are able to take place within the body of the recipient.

All healing is administered by specialists in the spirit world who diagnose the condition of the patient and perform the appropriate treatments. The subtle body acts as a blueprint for what takes place on the physical level. As a result many diseases manifest first on an energetic level before developing physically. Traditional Oriental medicine, Ayurvedic medicine, and similar healing systems recognize this by using a holistic approach to treatment that unblocks and balances the life energies of the patient resulting in physical cures and improvements.

Spiritual healing is the same in that it treats the whole person; body, mind and soul. Spiritual healing may be applied through direct laying on of the hands involving physical contact with the body of the patient or varying degrees of connecting through the energy fields of the patient. One of the greatest proponents of spiritual healing was the British trance medium and healer Harry Edwards, who authored some of the most comprehensive books on the subject and for decades widely, publicized spiritual healing throughout the UK.

Edwards emphasized simplicity and taught that physical technique was second to attunement of the healer with the healing source, or God. Edwards taught that the position of the hands during healing did not matter, a healer could have his or her hands in his or her pockets and, if properly attuned, the healing would take place. According to Edwards and many other experienced healers, some of the best results take place with people at distance through absent or distant healing.

Healing is a phase of mediumship often overlooked by many mediums. When I first started to study mediumship in the Spiritualist church setting, I was surprised that many experienced mediums did not work with hands-on healing. The practice of spiritual healing is important when it comes to mediumistic development for two major reasons.

First, it gives students of mediumship the right motivation for wanting to work with mediumship. The only ingredient necessary for any form of spiritual healing is love and the desire to help others. All mediumship is an act of love. Love motivates the spirit loved ones and the higher guides to want to communicate and connect with people in the physical world. In order to be a genuinely effective instrument for the spirit world the medium must be motivated completely by love and not by the desire for recognition or material gain.

Second, the practice of spiritual healing is often a stepping stone to the development of other phases of spirit communication. When working with spiritual healing the student learns to mentally disassociate and achieves varying degrees of altered consciousness. The process of channeling healing energy combined with hands-on contact with the energy fields and physical body of the recipient leads to greater awareness of spirit.

Many UK mediums believe the practice of spiritual healing should be kept separate from mental mediumship as demonstrated in circles or public meetings. They are convinced that the psychic energies involved are best utilized when focused on one aspect of mediumship. Typically, Spiritualist churches in the UK do not include hands-on healing as part of their regular public services. In the USA, it is the opposite, with spiritual healing treatments included in worship services. The inclusion of spiritual healing with mental mediumship always results in creating a more powerful level of energy and educationally as noted assists students open up even more with their natural abilities.

Spiritual healing is *God's love in action.* Although the personal life force energies of the healer are involved such energies are not transferred to the recipient. Instead the healing medium acts as a vehicle for higher frequencies of healing energies to pass through for the benefit of the recipient.

All healing is a planned act and operates under the direction of the spirit doctors and healers who work through the energy field of the medium to connect with the physical and subtle energy systems of the recipient. The spirit doctors generally come from a background of involvement with healing and might have worked as a surgeon, nurse or Native American Indian medicine person when they were in the physical world. The compassion in their hearts combined with a strong motivation to help others in the physical world leads such personalities to continue their studies and involvement with healing in the spirit world.

Spirit healers are attracted to working with healers in the physical world who possess a similar mindset and desire to serve those suffering mentally and physically. Through clairvoyance or clairsentience, often spirit doctors may be discerned within the energy field of the healer administering the treatment to the recipient. Mediumistic healers, as they gain experience, will also gradually learn to detect the presence of the spirit healers working with them through clairsentient awareness.

As with other phases of mediumship, the process of spiritual healing involves teamwork between the medium and the group of healers in the spirit world assisting them. Such healers are all specialists in various aspects of healing and based on the needs of the recipient will work through the medium accordingly. This is similar to patients with a health issue initially consulting a general practitioner and then being referred to other medical specialists.

Many people are natural healers and give off their own vital energy without even realizing it. This is wonderful in that the disposition to help others is there and consequently others who are depleted physically or emotionally will feel recharged after being in their physical presence

Spiritual healing should never be exhausting but should always invigorate the healer. A healer using only his or her life force energy will end up feeling drained. In addition, many such natural healers lack energetic boundaries, and often take on the physical and emotional conditions of others, which only detrimentally affects them. Many nurses, massage therapists, mental health specialists, and others involved as caregivers, possess the psychological disposition of wanting to rescue others and save them. In order to be an effective channel for spiritual healing, healers must learn to establish strong energetic boundaries between themselves and the people they work with as well as develop the ability to raise their own vibration and get themselves out-of-the-way in order for higher frequencies of energy to be channeled through them.

The only major skill needed to work with spiritual healing is the ability to attune to the healing source, which is accomplished by regular meditation and prayer. Pick up any *New Age* magazine and one will find many advertisements for training in various approaches to energy healing. Even the *Reiki* system of healing, developed by a Japanese medium in the last century, has countless variations being offered by various instructors. Students of healing attend such training and instead of learning how to raise their own vibrations and connect to the healing source, they are often burdened by acquiring an assortment of techniques that actually inhibit them from achieving proper attunement. Conscious effort regarding technique may impede the healer's attunement and weaken his or her connection with the healing source.

It is important to remember that healing is not a franchise and the development of healing goes beyond an external technique acquired through a certificate program. Formal study is essential in that it enables the healer to understand the mechanics of the process as well as professionally know how to interact with patients. However, the gift of healing is found within the heart and cannot be purchased for any price as it is acquired through the soul-growth and compassion of the healer.

Many of the Shamanic forms of spiritual healing involve ritual and ceremony as part of the healing process. Some approaches to healing involve healing passes or actions within the energy field, while others require specific hand positions directly on the physical body of the recipient. These motions and techniques are secondary to the attunement of the healer.

When I work with healing I mentally pray and ask that God heal the recipient for his or her highest good and growth body, mind and soul. I aim to keep myself in a prayerful and meditative state for the duration of the healing session. Physical touch is not absolutely necessarily as part of the treatment, but sometimes recipients will be more receptive if the hands are placed at the location of the discomfort. Spiritual healing may be effectively combined with massage and other forms of physical therapies and treatments. As all healing comes from God healing works hand in hand with all forms of medicine.

During my first visit to India I was blessed with the opportunity of meeting and interviewing Dr. Ramakant Keni, a leading medical doctor and major proponent of spiritual healing in India. It was incredible to see the large number of individuals waiting to receive spiritual healing at his office in Mumbai Hospital. Many of his patients had traveled considerable distance for treatment of extreme health conditions not generally found in more developed countries like the USA.

I have known other mediums, who also held qualifications as medical professionals, who were able to combine the practice of spiritual healing with other healing modalities and mainstream medical treatments. At one point, at least *one-third* of the students actively attending my mediumship development classes were mental health professionals: counselors, psychotherapists, psychiatric nurses and social workers. All were interested in learning spiritual healing in order to assist their patients.

The mechanics of healing involve the blending of the energy fields of the healer and the recipient. It is through the physical and energetic contact of the healer that the spirit doctors are able to diagnose the conditions of the recipient and also administer the appropriate healing treatment.

Healing is not just about physical cures or fixing a particular part of the physical body. The physical body will ultimately cease to function with the soul continuing to exist in the spirit dimension. Most diseases of the physical body are caused largely by disharmony and imbalances within the mind. The spirit doctors are less interested in mending the physical body and more concerned with spiritually touching our hearts. They seek to make us aware of our true eternal nature as spirit. The seemingly miraculous alleviation of physical ailments demonstrate the reality of spirit power and that life is more than merely the temporary material world.

While healing, the healer's physical and subtle energy bodies act as a transformer for the higher frequencies of healing energy being channeled through him or her. The spirit doctors work in a number of ways on the subtle and physical systems of the patient. First, they will unblock and balance the meridians or channels that circulate life energy throughout the physical body. Oriental medicine similarly focuses on bringing harmony to the physical body through acupuncture, massage and other techniques. Much of what takes during a healing is preventive and on an energetic level. Disease always manifests first on a subtle level.

Healing treatments are holistic. The spirit doctors simultaneously work on the subtle and physical bodies of the recipient. During treatment the recipients mind achieves a deep, peaceful state of body and mind. Emotional blocks and issues stored on deeper levels of the unconscious are also released as needed.

The spirit doctors also on some occasions directly remove physical matter such as cancerous tissue or arthritic deposits from the physical body of the recipient resulting in physical cures taking place. In physical mediumship, the spirit chemists, under the right conditions, are able to dematerialize physical objects and teleport them to the seance room, where they are materialized and presented to the seance attendees as gifts. This phase of physical mediumship known as *apportation* is produced by the spirit healers in the same manner, but instead for the purpose of dynamic physical healing.

In the Philippines some healing mediums under the control of their spirit doctors insert their fingers and hands directly into the patient's physical body as part of the healing procedure. This remarkable and controversial approach to spiritual healing is known as psychic surgery. Similarly, in Brazil and other locations there are mediums entranced by spirit doctors who perform operations on unanesthetized patients using knives and other instruments.

Patients receiving healing typically experience a sense of great inner calmness and joy and a stronger connection with God. Sensations of heat or cold as well as other sensations within the energy field and upon the physical body are also commonly experienced by the recipient. In some cases, recipients may feel as though they are physically touched or even physically worked on inside their bodies.

Etheric injections administered by the spirit doctors may also be experienced with recipients literally feeling as though they are injected physically with a syringe. In the Philippines some of the healing mediums are controlled by the spirit doctors to make the physical motion of an injection with their hands resulting with patients actually experiencing the sensation of a needle penetrating their skin. A student of mine, sitting in a mediumship development circle, once clairvoyantly received the vivid impression of a large orange carrot followed by the feeling of a needle being stuck into her eye. This particular student possessed extremely poor vision being both near and farsighted.

Healing always works, not necessarily with a physical cure, but it always touches recipients spiritually and assists them for their highest good and growth. I have taught many students over the years trained in *Reiki* or similar systems of energy work. It does not matter what system a person studies or the physical technique employed as the spirit healers work through anyone who sincerely desires to help those in need.

During a *Reiki* treatment often the recipient lies on a massage table while the healer places his or her hands all over the physical body. While I enjoy receiving healing lying down, not everyone is comfortable in such a vulnerable position. In most Spiritualist centers patients receive healing seated on a chair or stool for a shorter duration of time than a full *Reiki* session, especially if the treatment is given during a public meeting.

Although healing is received instantly and longer sessions are not necessary for achieving effective results, I feel that spending more time with the recipients is good as it provides more time for them to relax their bodies and go deep within themselves. In such a tranquil state they naturally become more receptive to the healing that is taking place.

Physical touch and nurturing are also important. While massage techniques generally are not combined with the process of spiritual healing as practiced in a formal Spiritualist church setting, I feel that the physical contact makes the healing more complete. Of course, people respond to physical touch differently and many people coming for hands-on healing are not comfortable with physical touch.

Important Points for Healers

- **Do not diagnosis or prescribe unless properly licensed to do so.** This is to protect the general public from quacks and unqualified practitioners. Medical doctors and nurse practitioners may legally diagnose and prescribe. Regardless if accurate information has been provided by the spirit world, healing mediums should avoid giving out such information.

- **Do not give spirit messages while working with healing.** It is best to be disciplined with mediumship as the patient is there to receive spiritual healing, not a spirit message. The attunement involved with spiritual healing is different from the type of attunement utilized to receive clairvoyant communications originating from spirit loved ones and guides. It is best for healers to focus on maintaining a meditative and prayerful state, while channeling healing energy and not attempt to psychically tune into patients or mediumistically receive communications for them.

- **Do not massage or manipulate.** Although we know healing on the direct area can be helpful, it is best practice in a church situation to keep physical contact shoulders and above. It is also important with the context of a church setting not to include massage or manipulation as part of the treatment. When moving hand positions on the physical body of the patient, the hands should never be brushed across the body of the patient as such an action would constitute massage. Instead they should be lifted and moved to the new position before making physical contact.

- **Always ask permission to touch the patient.** Never force healing and never place the hands on a part of the patients physical body that would cause embarrassment or make him or her feel uncomfortable. I have observed many well-meaning, sincere healers touch patients all over the physical body, an unwise practice leading to potential embarrassment or even trauma for some patients and litigation for the healer. Should the patient feel uneasy with physical contact, work within the energy field. Healers should also position and keep their physical bodies an arm's length from the body of the patient. Do not lean in or make any physical contact with the patient

- **Any physical touch should be kept light.** Hands should never be pressed on the top of the head or elsewhere with a level of pressure that may feel uncomfortable for the patient. I remember an elderly medium who worked with healing during the services of a Spiritualist church that I once pastored. At the close of the healing he would loudly proclaim to the recipient, "Go with God!" while forcefully dropping his hands on his or her shoulders. The patient in a deep meditative state would be startled and jump out of his or her seat when hit in this manner by his hands. The church had many large, overhead ceiling fans and it is surprising that no decapitations took place.

- **Be a healer not an actor.** Avoid mannerisms that detract from the simplicity of the process and draw unnecessary attention toward the healer. I have witnessed healers loudly pray as they administered the healing, while waving their arms in wild, theatrical motions.

- **Be well-groomed and properly dressed.** Presentation and personal hygiene are everything. A ketchup stained tee-shirt, garlic smelling hands and extreme body odor is no way going to help the patient be receptive to the healing vibrations.

- **Keep information about the patient confidential.** Unless the patient is a danger to themselves or others, the healer should refrain from discussing details about the patient with others. Harry Edwards stated that the healer has a responsibility to the patient, the healing gift and God. Ethically the healer should have high standards and respect the privacy of their patients, have reverence toward the healing process with the understanding that ultimately all healing comes from God.

- **Keep professional boundaries.** Do not flirt with patients or attempt to seduce them. All dealings with patients should be completely professional with boundaries being kept. In most cases, it is good for healers to have someone physically present when working with patients of the opposite sex. Minors should also not be treated except with the permission of their parent or guardian.

In general, the laws governing healing vary between regions and the healer should familiarize themselves with what is acceptable in terms of approaches to healing treatments. Even within the Spiritualist movement the practice of healing in terms of format and techniques vary greatly depending upon the location. A good healer is able to modify their technique and application according to time and circumstances. The do's and don'ts described above are not written in stone, but are practical considerations suggested primarily for the benefit and comfort of the recipients of hands-on spiritual healing.

Spiritual Healing Step By Step

- **1.** Introduce yourself to the patient and briefly explain the procedure for hands-on spiritual healing as well as ask permission to touch the patient while administering treatment. While it is unnecessary to know anything about the patient, for the purpose of building positive rapport and trust, a talk beforehand helps create better receptivity as well as enables the healer to better understand how to best approach and help the patient.

- **2.** Place hands on the shoulders of the seated patient and silently pray asking to be used as an healing instrument for the highest good of the patient.

- **3.** Allow your hands to be guided within the aura as well as placed upon the physical body of the patient. Temperature changes are commonly experienced at different parts of the patient's physical body. It is best to remain in a meditative and prayer state while healing, instead of attempting to psychically tune into the patient. A properly attuned healer allows the power to flow and be directed to the patient.

- **4.** Develop an internal sense of when to bring the healing to a close. Gratitude to the healing source should always be given.

Say, "God bless you," and gently touch the shoulders of the patient to let him or her know the healing treatment is over.

A formal beginning and end for each session is essential as it helps the recipient achieve a sense of comfort by feeling the physical and spiritual presence of the healer. Many healers position their hands gently on the shoulders of the patient. I have experienced healers begin and end the healing process without any physical contact and in some cases verbal closing. Such an approach is not best for creating a safe, nurturing environment conducive for healing and leaves the patient feeling unsure of what is going on in terms of the healing.

Absent Healing

Absent healing is the process of requesting through prayer and intention that healing be directed by God with the assistance of the spirit healers to recipients at a distance from the healer. When practicing absent healing the healer goes into the same prayerful state as when practicing hands on healing. While in a state of attunement the healer may mentally or quietly verbalize the names of people in need of healing and ask God with the assistance of the spirit doctors to heal those being prayed for mentally, physically and spiritually.

Dowsing the Aura Exercises

These exercises require a pair of dowsing rods, which may be constructed out of metal coat hangers or bent copper wire. There are many places where dowsing rods are available for purchase online or by order from various dowsing organizations. Dowsing rods, once energetically connected, become a psychic extension of the individual's energy fields responding to external stimuli in the same manner as the aura normally does. All the dowsing sensitivity exercises that follow are best done in an area with large space.

EXERCISE 75

Sensing the Aura with Dowsing Rods

Participant holding dowsing rods slowly approaches subject sitting in chair from various distances stopping at the location that the dowsing rods react. This exercise may be repeated with different individuals sitting in the chair. It clearly demonstrates to the student doing the exercise as well as those observing the measurable dimensions of the energy fields. When done in a group ideally all the members should work with the rods with as many seated subjects as possible.

EXERCISE 76

Sensing the Layers of the Aura with Dowsing Rods

This exercise is the same as the previous exercise only that the participant attempts to locate, while holding the dowsing rods, the emotional, mental and spiritual layers of the aura. The physical layer lies close to the body and is not detectable with dowsing rods, but the emotional, mental and spiritual layers are easily discernible. The same procedures and approach as described in the previous dowsing rod exercise may be applied to this exercise.

EXERCISE 77

Dowsing Expanded Aura

The seated subject's energy field will be measured by participant using the dowsing rods. The instructor requests the subject to deliberately expand their energy field. The participant again uses the dowsing rods to measure the difference in size. The subject may also be requested to withdraw his or her energy field closer to the physical body with the results measured through use of the dowsing rods. As with the previous dowsing rod exercises, this exercise should be repeated with as many subjects as possible.

EXERCISE 78

Depleted Aura-Before and After Healing

The teacher selects a member of the group who is physically or mentally exhausted and places him or her in a seat. A participant with dowsing rods proceeds to measure the distance of the subject's aura. The subject next receives spiritual healing and after which a participant measures the difference in size of the energy field as a result of the healing. This exercise may be done even with people not greatly depleted energetically or exhausted as it demonstrates the changes that take place.

EXERCISE 79

Dowsing during Healing

Participants break into groups of three with one using the dowsing rods, while the other two pair up and take turns giving and receiving spiritual healing. The participant utilizes the dowsing rods to determine the increased size of the energy fields of those involved during the process of spiritual healing. Members of the group can switch roles, so each gets an opportunity to work with the dowsing rods as well as give and receive healing.

EXERCISE 80

Dowsing Charged Water

Participant with dowsing rods measures reaction of rods to container of water placed on ground. Next, the container of water is charged with healing energy by several healers who hold it, while praying and directing energy into the water. The participant with dowsing rods again measures the reaction of rods to the container with water. The difference with the water before and after should be apparent demonstrating the effect of healing upon water.

EXERCISE 81

Blindfolded Dowsing

A participant blindfolded with dowsing rods attempts to find with the rods containers of water placed at various locations on the floor or ground. While the blindfolded will be unable to see the rods react to the water, students observing this exercise will clearly see the reaction.

Medical Intuition Exercises

It is important to note that in many places in the world it is illegal to diagnosis or prescribe unless one is licensed as a physician. Individuals told of potentially severe or even minor health conditions may experience great anxiety or anguish. Students performing these exercises should keep in mind the educational nature and purpose of these exercises and not hold back in relating the health conditions they intuitively discern.

Remember that students of psychic development are in the process of learning and regularly misinterpret psychic information and get their own minds in the way. If someone does not feel comfortable with these exercises, then he or she should not participant.

EXERCISE 82

Medical Scan

A subject, who is aware of their physical health conditions, is seated in front of the group. After a brief guided meditation for attunement to healers in the spirit world, participants mentally attempt to tune into the subject and discern physical and mental imbalances or disorders. Participants are encouraged to use their own intuitive ability to pick up on conditions as well as information received from spirit doctors in the spirit world. The teacher will suggest that participants observe the aura objectively with their physical eyes, mentally scan the body of the subject, trust their gut feelings and notice other ways in which the information might come through

Participants share information as they receive it. The subject does not provide any feedback, until the conclusion of the exercise. This exercise may be done with more than one person as the subject. The more severe the health conditions, the easier it will be for students to psychically discern the conditions. Subjects who are aware of their physical health history and current status are ideal as they can provide detailed feedback in response to the input of the participants.

EXERCISE 83

Medical Scan with Drawing

Participants pair up and sit in rows across from each other; one partner acting as the subject with the other working to scan the body. The teacher leads a short meditation to connect participants doing the scanning with their spirit doctors and suggests that they mentally tune into the subject seated across from them. The teacher tells participants to see the subject's body within their minds as a transparent form and to scan the body from head to toe, paying close attention to areas that may indicate disease or disharmony.

As they scan the subject's body participants may note distinct colors or energetic build up in various regions of the anatomy. Participants need to trust their intuition and determine the meaning of what they are discerning in terms of past or present health conditions.

Participants are brought back from the meditation and use colored markers or crayons to vividly depict their partner's physical body, aura and what is being discerned. Information is not limited to being obtained only through clairvoyance and clairsentience but may be received mediumistically through hearing, smelling, tasting or knowing.

Upon completing the drawing and sharing with the subject and others in the group, the subject provides feedback to the best of his or her ability. The exercise may be repeated with the participants switching roles.

EXERCISE 84

Scanning the Body with Fingers

Participants divide into pairs with one seated or lying down and the other working to scan the body using the fingers. The emphasis in this exercise is sensing the physical layer of the aura which energetically is the densest auric emanation and reflects the physical health of the subject.

Participants place their hands at the top of their partner's head and, with their hands close to the physical body, slowly sweep their hands all the way down to the toes. The fingers should remain at all times within the aura of the subject and at no point touch the physical body. This motion should be done relatively slow, not for the purpose of transmitting healing energy or curative force, but for the purpose of discerning though subtle sensation the physiological conditions of the subject. Participants should feel as though they are seeing and feeling with their fingers being aware of every slight sensation, variation in temperature, and density of energy that they feel.

Particular attention should be paid at the location of the major chakras or energy centers as well as the major physical organs and glands. If the subject is in a reclined position the scanning may be done as necessary on the front of the body before having the subject turn over to repeat the process on the back. Participants should share their findings as they work with the subject, who will not provide any feedback or confirmation of the details given. At the end of exercise feedback may be given and partners can switch roles and repeat the exercise.

Chapter 15

Past Life Readings

As the embodied soul continuously passes, in this body, from boyhood to youth to old age, the soul similarly passes into another body at death. A sober person is not bewildered by such a change.

(Bhagavad-Gita 2.13)

The soul is eternal and continues to function after the physical body is destroyed. Every soul incarnates in a physical body that is based on its level of consciousness and suitable for the particular environment that it inhabits. Spirit communication, as a process, proves the reality of life after death. Generally, Individuals falsely identify with their physical bodies and minds believing that the face they see in the mirror is their real self, yet the face ages along with the other parts of the physical body with every cell and molecule changing completely on the average of every seven years.

There are many intelligent people who are in denial about life after death. Such misguided individuals mistakenly believe that they are their physical body and mind, a result of chemicals being mixed together in the right combination to create life. It goes without saying that people who do not accept their true spiritual nature and the reality of life after death are in for a rude awakening.

Investigating psychic phenomena in an open-minded and intelligent manner leads to the development of complete conviction in the survival of consciousness after physical death. However, acceptance of mediumship does necessarily mean acceptance of reincarnation or physical rebirth after the destruction of the physical body. Many people involved with the practice of mediumship consider reincarnation to be an unproven theory. After all, with mediumship facts regarding deceased individuals, even if not understood at the time, may ideally be researched and validated. A medium could tell a person all sorts of things about an alleged past life, but in general such information rarely may be effectively researched to prove that what has come through is factually correct.

As a medium I have absolutely no problem accepting reincarnation as a fact. The understanding of reincarnation is found in many cultures worldwide with the most scientific and comprehensive explanations found in the Vedic literature originating in ancient India. I highly recommend that individuals interested in learning about the mechanics of reincarnation and the process of changing bodies, study the Bhagavad-gita and other Vedic scriptures as the spiritual laws governing the soul, and its entanglement in matter, are thoroughly explained in a practical manner.

As a medium I have experienced vivid memories of what I know were my past lives and I have also received accurate information through other mediums about my previous incarnations. During a mediumship session with my teacher, Pauline Hathaway, at the Church of Two Worlds, she described seeing me as a Native American Indian healer who worked with prayers and massage in a cave in the region that is now California, long before the Europeans settled the area. A week later, I attended a home circle at Sylvia's house and her husband Joseph received a message, in which he saw me as a Native American Indian healer in a cave with pouches of herbal preparations hanging from the ceiling. Both mediums essentially described a similar vision of the exact scene, with many of the same details, within a week of each other.

In my work as medium, I have many times received similar communications from the spirit world about the past lives of individuals who come to me for sessions. I do not receive such information all the time, but when it comes through the details are relevant to the recipient in terms of issues or patterns in their present lives.

For example, I once did a mediumship session for a woman who was heavily involved in healing and spiritual growth. It was revealed by the guides that in a past life she had been incredibly ruthless and responsible for the slaughter of many innocent people. Even though she had gone through other physical lives and changed, she still blamed herself for what she had done.

In her desire to make up for her past misdeeds, she tended to be especially hard on herself, despite the fact that she was completely devoted to healing and helping others. Although the time and place of the past incarnation were not revealed by the guides, its effects upon her general psychological and behavioral patterns made great sense to her.

In another session, I channeled information about a past life for a young woman that significantly affected her present disposition. The guides showed her as a religious fanatic and zealous member of a cult that was considered heretical, led by a charismatic leader. The extreme views held by the members of this group resulted in them being burned to death. The trauma of this horrible experience left, on a soul level, a great feeling of betrayal for blindly following this particular leader as part of the group. In her present life she intensely mistrusted cults and organized religions and, in general, did not want to get intimately involved in such groups or follow the instructions of spiritual leaders.

During a session that I gave to another young woman, I was shown a past life at the time of the Spanish *Armada*, in England. She was in a male body and locked up in a prison and never released. According to the information that came through, there was no justifiable reason for her confinement, and the hopelessness of the situation, with no way to be released or ever to experience freedom, greatly affected her on a soul level in ways that considerably influenced her psychological and behavioral patterns in the present.

This same young woman, as a toddler, had dreams, of trench warfare during the First World War. I remember being told by the guides during another session that I did for her that she had physically died in the First World War as I was shown fighter planes from that era and the battlefields and trenches in Europe.

The study of past lives is fascinating. The better we understand ourselves the more we overcome negative patterns of thinking and behavior that hold us back from greater happiness and personal expansion. As with all forms of psychic phenomena, I suggest that caution always be used when presented with information given by mediums or psychics about alleged past lives.

Most past life information is too distant or impractical to properly research. However, the higher guides involved in providing such details will attempt to validate the past lives through different mediums. In addition, they may also attempt to induce spontaneous recollection of memories of particular past lives. Genuine past life memories are vivid and accompanied by feelings associated with the details of the particular life and time period.

The best way to develop the ability as a medium to receive past life details for others is to sincerely desire to help people through conveying this type of information and to ask the higher guides to provide it. In my experience as a medium, past life information does not come through all the time, but when it does, it is relevant to the present life of the individual and generally relates to issues or patterns affecting his or her present life.

Spiritualists, who do not accept the concept of reincarnation, argue that past life information coming through mediumistically is actually a description of spirit personalities presently around the recipient, whom are misunderstood by the medium to be past lives of the person receiving the communication. I do not agree with this explanation, since details about past life identities of individuals presently incarnate completely differ from mediumistically connecting with the living energy of a personality in the spirit world.

It is a fact that the soul is eternal and physical rebirth is a natural process governed by higher dimensional laws. If we want to know about our past incarnations, we should not consult a medium for answers, but instead closely examine our present situation as it is a direct result of our past actions in this and previous lives. We should ask ourselves; "What are my faults and shortcomings on a personal level?" The character flaws we presently possess are issues that need to be resolved for the law of Karma or cause and effect is perfect.

The information conveyed through me from higher teachers in the spirit world has consistently validated these points. As eternal spiritual personalities, we are responsible for our own happiness and misery and through our materialistic desires to enjoy separately from God, we take physical birth repeatedly. The higher guidance and wisdom received mediumistically enables us to respond to the challenges of material life from a position of elevated consciousness. Past life details provided by our spiritual guardians through mediumistic communications empower us to move beyond negative patterns of thinking and behavior that hold us back from greater awareness of God and self.

CHAPTER 16

Self-Development for Mediums

The source of any spirit message does not originate with the medium but with the world of spirit. A medium is only an instrument for the spirit personalities to work through. There are many different mediums with varying skills and abilities as mediums. The nature of the messages that individual mediums are able to bring through depends not only upon their natural talent, training, and experience, but also very much on the spiritual and mental vibrations of the particular medium and the harmonious connection established with the communicating spirits.

Some mediums are better suited for certain types of messages as they resonate with spirits of a similar wavelength. Mediumship is not about being better or worse. A spirit message that is accurately delivered is all that matters. Too often, mediums are judged by others, especially other mediums, based on their performance or the details of the message that they have conveyed.

Fault Finding and Jealousy

I have observed over the years the tendency on the part of many mediums to criticize and find fault with the work of other mediums.

"That wasn't evidential" or "His mediumship isn't very good" are statements commonly made by mediums after watching other mediums publicly work or even receiving a private session.

While there are certainly superior methods or presentation skills for demonstrating mediumship in public, and poor training and lack of experience typically lead to greater error and distortion, it is better for mediums to refrain from criticizing the work of other mediums. Positive, constructive input is one thing, but, in a general sense, the tendency to find fault in the work of others is due to insecurities and wanting to make ourselves seem and feel better. Fault finding and negative criticism is one way of doing this at the expense of others.

The late Ursula Roberts, a British trance medium and healer, who wrote many excellent books on mediumship development, emphasized that mediums need to guard themselves against the danger of criticizing other mediums. According to Roberts, such criticism had to do with jealousy and the moment a medium found themselves doing so they should stop immediately. I had the good fortune of meeting Roberts at an International Spiritualist Congress in the UK a few years before her passing. Unlike many toxic and dysfunctional mediums, Roberts attempted to apply higher spiritual principles and philosophy in terms of how she lived her life in the material world.

Mediumship is not about attention or recognition. We should not feel important that others are impressed with our ability to bring through deceased loved ones or incredibly accurate information and guidance to help people with their lives. Mediums need to honestly examine their motivations for working with spirit communication.

Reasons Not to Become a Medium

- *I want to develop mediumship so I can impress people.*
- *I like to talk about how evidential and accurate my mediumship is.*
- *When observing other mediums publicly work, I find faults and things to criticize about their mediumship.*

- *I want to be a world-famous medium.*
- *I secretly desire adoration and attention from others.*
- *I want to be the star of a mediumship television show.*
- *I count how many pieces of evidential information that I bring through with my mediumship and tell everyone about it.*
- *I approach people in shopping malls, fast-food restaurants and other public places and give them spirit messages.*
- *My spirit teachers and guides are advanced masters.*
- *I have a special mission with my mediumship which distinguishes me from other people.*
- *Secretly, I feel happy when other mediums fail with their mediumship.*
- *Most other mediums are not working the right way with their mediumship.*
- *I want to be the center of attention.*
- *I am proud of my abilities as a medium.*

Qualities Necessary for Mediums

Love, empathy, high ethical standards, and compassion for others are qualities necessary for mediums. A spiritual medium is an instrument for higher spirit personalities to reach people in need in the physical world. Mediums should be motivated by love and a desire to selflessly give from their hearts

It is important for mediums to possess healthy self-esteem and psychological balance. Self-love and confidence also need to be present in order to be strong instruments for the spirit world and to effectively minister to those undergoing suffering and difficulties in the physical world. But there is a vast difference between emotionally feeling good about one's self and vanity. Negative beliefs about one's self lead to a lack of confidence and focus.

In order to function as a medium, there must be mental discipline and determination. Mediums who criticize the performance of other mediums demonstrate a profound weakness as true psychological strength is indicated by humility and acceptance of other people's imperfections.

George Lawton, psychologist and direct student of Sigmund Freud, researched the Spiritualist movement in 1929 as part of his doctoral dissertation for Columbia University in New York. He interviewed and psychologically analyzed many mediums and actively studied the movement by attending conventions, meetings, seances and workshops held at the Lily Dale Assembly in New York and elsewhere.

In 1932 he published his doctoral thesis, *The Drama of Life After Death: A Study of the Spiritualist Religion,* which remains one of the most comprehensive, independent studies of the Spiritualist movement and the psychological nature of its adherents. In Lawton's view, based on his direct observations over the period of his research, the typical medium was an uneducated nobody, who had not accomplished much with his or her life and used the practice of mediumship as a means of achieving greater importance and prominence among his or her peers.

The development of mediumship is all about self-growth and spiritual mastery, or at least it should be. Many people get involved in mediumship for the purpose of developing their psychic ability and acquiring mystic powers that psychologically will give them distinction and make them stand out from others. The idea that cultivating psychic ability or mediumship is the same as developing personal spirituality is false as there is a big difference between the two.

Spiritual growth is about developing one's relationship with God, spiritual character and applying spirituality in a practical sense in all aspects of life. Psychic abilities and mediumistic powers are wonderful and they are natural functions that can be cultivated through proper training. One can be an extremely unhealthy individual, emotionally and physically, and work effectively as a medium. Many mediums do not take care of their physical bodies or emotional health. However, the development of mediumship does not make any individual more spiritually evolved than others anymore than learning classical ballet or oil painting.

A Healthy Diet and Mediumship

We are what we eat. All food substances besides containing physical nutrients on a subtle level are composed of energies that affect our minds and bodies. Fresh fruits, vegetables, nuts, grains and beans are ideal as they contain the physical nutrients for superior health but also sufficient quantities of life energy. It is for these reasons that the Yogic tradition recommends a vegetarian diet for its adherents as such pure foods nourish the physical body, but also create a calm, serene state of mind conducive for higher meditative states.

The flesh of slaughtered animals should be avoided at all costs for not only is meat unhealthy contributing to many diseases and disorders that affect the physical body, but on a subtle level the fear and pain of the slaughtered animals is absorbed into the flesh. Anyone eating meat also is absorbing this destructive, negative energy.

The Yogic tradition also emphasizes the cultivation of compassion toward others and nonviolence. Eating meat contributes to the violent, painful slaughter of billions of innocent animals worldwide as well as the destruction of the Earth's environment. The natural laws of the universe are stringent, and when we live in disharmony with these laws, we suffer the appropriate reactions. The killing involved in animal slaughter is disharmonious and creates negative karma or reactions for those who eat meat and society as a whole. Many mediums regularly consume fast-food burgers and similar unhealthy foods, unconscious of the violence inflicted upon the animals, whose lives were cruelly taken, and the negative effects of eating dead flesh, upon their own physical health.

A vegetarian or vegan diet is highly recommended for mediums and healers. Pure vegetarians eat no meat, fish, eggs or products derived from such substances. Vegans additionally refrain from dairy products in their diet as well. A raw food diet is also worth considering as both the physical nutrients and life energy are not depleted as with cooked or processed foods. It is also ideal to eat organic food as much as possible too.

Eating meat and junk food also clogs up the energy meridians or channels as detailed in Chinese and other systems of Asian medicine. Try following a healthier diet and notice the difference in how you feel mentally and physically. The etheric body will operate at a higher frequency and overall the energy channels will be much clearer along with greater mental clarity.

Most people are raised consuming meat as a source of food and do not think that there is anything wrong with it. Many religions theologically justify eating animal flesh and some denominations of Christianity go as far as saying that there is no soul within the body of the animal. When vegetarianism is brought up many people naturally feel defensive and come up with excuses and rationalizations in support of their meat-eating. In terms of mediumship you can be a wonderful medium and eat meat, but psychically and spiritually it is much better to give it up.

Meat contains bad energy. If you do not believe this then perform a simple experiment and see for yourself. Take a pendulum and test the energy of meat compared to fresh fruit and vegetables. The proof is in the pudding as the life force within the former will be stronger and more vibrant than the flesh of slaughtered animals. Great spiritual teachers in the physical world as well as as higher spirit teachers such as Silver Birch and White Eagle, the spirit teacher of the late British Trance Medium Grace Cook, advocate a meatless diet based on love and compassion.

The Physical Body is God's Temple

Addictive habits such as smoking and drinking alcohol should be avoided, as they pollute the physical body as well as the subtle energy fields. When I first got involved in the study of mediumship, I noticed how many mediums smoked cigarettes. Sadly, quite a few passed over due to health conditions caused directly by this deadly addiction.

"It's not what you put in what matters, it's what you think,"*gasped* one of my students, who had been chastised by another participant in a mediumship development class I was teaching for smoking a cigarette outside during the break. While I understood her point about the power of the mind over our physical health, the fact that she was extremely overweight with a serious respiratory condition that made her *gasp* for air with practically every breath did not give support to her argument.

The physical body is the temple for the Divine and we should care for it properly. Regardless of how positive our thoughts may be, inhaling smoke is not a loving action and contributes greatly in injuring our physical body as well as the physical bodies of those around us.

Exercise the Physical Body

Regular physical exercise is important for practicing mediums as are subtle exercises for the cultivation of life energy and physical health. Hatha yoga, qi-gong, traditional martial arts and related disciplines are all excellent in assisting mediums maintain physical health, calm the nervous system, and purify the energy channels of the subtle body.

Physical massage and bodywork are beneficial to regularly receive as such treatments ground recipients and bring them back into their physical bodies. Since mental mediumship greatly stimulates the nervous system, any physical activity that brings about a peaceful state of mind and soothes the nerves should be practiced by the medium. Even causal activities such as taking walks or gardening are highly beneficial. A medium should spend as much time around nature as possible.

I also recommend practicing mediums involve themselves in doing some sort of artistic or musical endeavor separate from their work as mediums. Creative activity is therapeutic, makes use of the imagination and frees up the intuitive mind

It is essential that mediums take care of themselves physically, mentally, emotionally and spiritually. If we want to be clear channels for the spirit world, we must know our defects and weaknesses and work through them, using whatever resources are available. If we need to see a therapist, attend a support group, or practice various self-help techniques, then it needs to done for unless we are healed within, we will be limited in the support that we give to others. We cannot give to others what we don't have ourselves.

If we are toxic in our thinking and lifestyle then how can we possibly be channels for the higher spiritual truths? Pornography and negative entertainment should be avoided as well as they pollute the unconscious mind and limit the spiritual light and goodness from flowing through.

How to Spiritualize Mediumship

An essential teaching received from higher spirit teachers is that we must take personal responsibility for our actions in the physical world and should treat others in the manner that we would like to be treated. The development of spiritual character, love of God, and soul-realization is the essence of all the world's major religious traditions. Psychic growth within itself will not result in higher God realization or improvement of personal character.

Mediums must learn to live their spirituality to the best of their ability through their thoughts, words and actions. The higher spirit teachers state that no matter how many mistakes we make while living in the physical world that we always have another opportunity to improve ourselves and learn from what we have done wrong. The doorway to reformation and personal improvement is never closed as we create, moment by moment, our own misery or happiness through the choices we make.

The Buddhist Precepts

Buddhism provides five basic precepts that when followed greatly enhance one's personal development and spiritualize one's mediumship. These suggestions for improvement are universal in nature and application of these precept's in one's daily life will optimize a happier and healthier experience.

The Buddhist precepts are;

1. Do not kill
2. Do not steal
3. Do not indulge in sexual misconduct
4. Do not make false speech
5. Do not take intoxicants

Prayer and Meditation

Prayer and meditation are essential for spiritual strength and purity. When we pray we talk to God and when we meditate we actively listen to God. There is a difference between meditating to connect with the presence of the Divine within the heart and to acquire psychic or mediumistic ability.

There are many approaches to prayer and meditation found within the world's religious traditions. Daily prayer and meditation should be part of every mediums standard routine. There are many benefits that result from daily practice physically, mentally and spiritually, but the most important benefit is the awareness of self and one's relationship with the Supreme Self.

Cleaning the Heart

Psychic science and mediumship demonstrate beyond a shadow of doubt the immortality of the individual soul or personality after the destruction of the physical body. Regular prayer and meditation clean all the dust that covers the mirror of the heart preventing us from seeing ourselves as pure spirit, eternally connected to God. This dust contains many negative, unwanted qualities, past trauma and unwanted programming from this physical life as well as previous incarnations. When the mirror is clear, we see within its reflection that we are eternal personalities.

Our physical and subtle bodies provide us with a false identity or role that we play in the physical world. Prayer helps to remove our false identification with the external, temporary physical world and understand our true spiritual nature.

The Power of Mantra Meditation

Some traditions such as Zen or Virnapassa Buddhism teach forms of silent meditation, in which the meditator learns to focus their awareness within. As a child I learned *Transcendental Meditation* (*TM*), which involved sitting quietly and mentally repeating a silent mantra. Years later, I learned to use a *japa mala* or rosary of prayer beads to chant sacred *mantras* for the purpose of developing devotion to God and gaining greater spiritual realization of self. In many traditions prayer beads are used by the religious practitioner to keep track of the number of prayers as well as to focus the sense of touch as part of the meditative process.

It is helpful to have a mantra or prayer that can be repeated silently or aloud as a means to focus the mind and go within. Sometimes people criticize such formal prayers as being mechanical or lacking the spontaneous feeling of praying in one's own words from ones heart. Prayer and meditation should never be a boring routine or mechanical and I know from my own personal experience that such mantras when sincerely prayed with love and devotion are excellent as a process to awaken higher consciousness.

The following are a sampling of mantra prayers used in several of the world's religious traditions for spiritual transformation and realization of God. The English translations are included as most of the prayers are recited in other languages.

Vedic

Hare Krishna, Hare Krishna, Krishna Krishna, Hare Hare
Hare Rama, Hare Rama, Rama, Rama, Hare Hare

Oh energy of the Lord, Oh all-attractive Lord, Oh Supreme Enjoyer, please engage me in Your service.

Buddhist

Namo Amitābhāya

Homage to the Infinite Light.

Christian

Hail Mary, full of grace, the Lord is with thee. Blessed art thou amongst women, and blessed is the fruit of thy womb, Jesus. Holy Mary, mother of God, pray for us sinners, now and at the hour of our death. Amen.

Islamic

Allahu Akbar

God is great.

What does the practice of mantra meditation have to do with mediumship? Regular mantra meditation spiritually purifies the mind of the medium and assists in the development of spirituality and personal character. Such spiritual qualities will naturally result in a higher vibration reflected in the energy fields surrounding the medium.

In the Yogic tradition mantras are also collectively chanted or sung with a group in a process known as *kirtan*. Individual mantra meditation is great, but it is even more powerful when such transcendental mantras are chanted with love and devotion in the company of others.

Mediums developing themselves spiritually in this manner will, through the Law of Attraction, attract higher level spirits to work through them. A high energetic, healthy lifestyle is essential for self-growth. The more we work on ourselves mentally, physically, emotionally and spiritually, the clearer and stronger we will be as instruments for the higher spirit personalities to work through.

Chapter 17

Dealing with Skeptics

When I lived in the Washington, DC area, I was fortunate to attend the annual conference of the Committee for the Scientific Investigation of Claims of the Paranormal (CSICOP), a rationalist and educational organization that has since changed its name to the Committee for Skeptical Inquiry (CSI). A regular reader of their journal, the *Skeptical Inquirer,* I found the conference quite intriguing as the focus was completely on debunking paranormal phenomena and pseudoscientific concepts, from UFOs to alternative forms of healing, such as acupuncture and homeopathy. I noticed that many of the conference attendees as well as individual speakers, such as magician and arch-skeptic, James Randi, seemed to be extremely closed off intuitively and out of touch with the energetic space around them. Standing next to *the Amazing Randi,* it was incredible to see how withdrawn his aura was from his physical body compared to the average person, whose energy fields tend to extend further in dimension.

According to a friend of mine, a Canadian medium and resident of the Lily Dale Assembly in New York, the late Paul Kurtz, the long time leader and founder of CSICOP, used to go to the Spiritualist community in disguise for sessions as part of his undercover investigations of mediumship. While Kurtz was a complete atheist and did not believe in an afterlife, his wife allegedly traveled regularly to Lily Dale for mediumship sessions.

Skepticism is a good thing and should be encouraged, as it is too easy, when it comes to mediumship, to be deluded and throw out all common sense. Unfortunately, as skeptics correctly observe, there is a high percentage of people, who will unquestioningly believe everything that a medium tells them regardless of how inaccurate or off the deep end it might be. As a medium I have brought through spirit personalities, describing them in detail, only to have the recipient attempt to change what I am saying, in order to make it fit the description of someone totally different in the spirit world, whom they want to hear from. Due to the general lack of discernment on the part of most people, it would be extremely easy to deceive people with mediumship by making things up or telling them what they want to hear.

Hardcore skeptics tend to be atheists and not open to the concept of spirit communication or anything having to do with spirituality. Not accepting the reality of life after death, they consider all mediums to be con-artists, deluded, or a combination of both. While most mediums will never have to deal with hardcore skeptics in an adversarial way, it is important that common arguments against mediumship utilized by skeptics be understood.

Cold Reading

Skeptics believe that much of what passes off as spirit communication involves use of cold reading techniques. According to them, the medium will throw out statements purporting to be from the spirit world based on the external appearance, background and reactions of the recipient. Often, the information will be worded as a question or in an ambiguous way that could apply to a high percentage of people or that would likely be accepted by the recipient. The medium will elaborate upon the hits giving the illusion that they are receiving the information from a discarnate source.

As a practicing medium for many years, I have observed very little conscious cold reading utilized by fraudulent mediums. Most of what I have witnessed could be considered unconscious cold reading with the individual thinking that they are receiving information from the spirit world, but instead coming up with material based on cues and input provided by the recipient. I think this sort of delusion happens quite frequently with untrained mediums, hence the need for higher educational standards in regards to mediumship training.

Shot Gunning

While cold reading might commonly be done slowly, the shot gunning technique involves the medium making a series of rapid-fire statements, often vague and generalized, some of which will likely be accepted by the recipient. Television medium John Edward has been accused by skeptics of this approach as he works on a fast vibration articulating the information that he receives quickly to the recipients of the communications. Although I do not ask questions during my delivery of spirit messages, I also work on a fast vibration and could be accused of the same thing by someone unaware of the mechanics of the process and predisposed to believing that mediumship is impossible.

Hot Reading

With hot reading the medium makes use of information acquired about the recipient and gives it to them making them think that it is being conveyed by the medium from the spirit world. Phony medium Lamar Keene's classic work, *The Psychic Mafia*, documents his experiences with the wide-spread sharing of information about clients within the Spiritualist community and the prevalence of fraudulent mediumship at Camp Chesterfield in Indiana and other Spiritualist centers. While most mediums are honest and ethical in their dealings, there are individuals who will cheat with their mediumship and obtain information about the people they are working with prior to the session.

Subjective Validation

In the view of the skeptics, subjective validation accounts for the main reason people are able to relate to information provided by mediums. Subjective validation is the tendency for people to somehow find a meaning or relationship within their own lives with the statements and details given by mediums. As with information provided by cold reading, details that cannot be made to somehow fit for the recipient, are overlooked in favor of the ones that do.

With subjective validation the recipients of purported spirit messages will fill in the blanks of statements made by the medium and make connections in order to make it somehow apply. As a practicing medium, I have observed this tendency firsthand, with people making what has been given to them have meaning, even when the information is incorrect or does not apply to them.

Warm Reading

Warm reading relies upon the subjective validation of the recipient and involves the medium giving purported spirit messages that seem specific and personal, yet in truth apply to many. The open-ended nature of the statements and the acceptance of them by the recipient allow the medium to completely manipulate the session creating the facade of genuine spirit communication taking place.

Coincidence

When the evidential statements made by a medium cannot be explained by subjective validation or cold, warm or hot reading, skeptics will chalk up such success as being the result of coincidence. After all, it is impossible to communicate with the dead as there is no survival of the personality after the destruction of the physical body.

Fraud and Delusion

As a whole skeptics view professional mediums with both contempt and suspicion, as they consider the practice of mediumship to be completely fraudulent. However, many recognize the obvious sincerity of the majority of people involved with mediumship and conclude that such individuals must be extremely deluded and in some cases suffering from visual and auditory hallucinations. Actually the skeptics are correct about this in regards to mediumship and delusion, as there are many sincere people working as mediums, who, lacking discernment and common sense, cannot tell the difference between thoughts originating from within their own minds and genuine psychic impressions.

Hardcore skeptics generally are extremely narrow-minded and regardless of the quality of evidence provided by a medium will always try to rationalize how the medium must have either cheated to obtain the information beforehand or utilized cold reading techniques to dupe the recipient. Over the years, I have had many atheists and skeptics come through as communicators for others during mediumship sessions. Disbelieve in an afterlife, does not change the fact that the personality survives physical death.

As a medium one of the biggest obstacles to successfully validating the reality of spirit communication is that it is very difficult to duplicate the results of experiments independently through the process of mechanistic science. I have participated in studies with the University of Virginia involving spirit communication and even did a mediumship session over the phone for Professor Gary Schwartz, best known for his groundbreaking work involving afterlife research at the University of Arizona.

The researchers I worked with were all open-minded and as such the chemistry present at the sessions was excellent producing favorable results. Schwartz in particular had requested, prior to his phone session with me, that a specific spirit person, whom he was involved in researching, come through. During the session the requested spirit personality conveyed much evidential information through me that Schwartz was able to identify. I was kept completely in the dark by Schwartz as to what I was talking about and how it related. In addition, all the researchers I have worked with were at least fairly knowledgeable about the mechanics of mediumship and how to obtain favorable results.

The average skeptic possesses insufficient comprehension of how the process works and as a result would not know how to properly conduct an investigation. Most skeptics have likely read few books on the subject and no experience consulting mediums or participating in mediumship development training programs.

With any form of spirit communication the psychic atmosphere affects the results. Many experiments involving mediums fail in terms of positive results due to the skeptical, disharmonious energies of the researcher, who damages the session unknowingly through his or her negative and closed mindset. Skeptics would counter this explanation stating that sympathetic, believers of psychic phenomena are more likely through subjective validation to accept statements given by mediums overlooking the parts that do not make sense or are inaccurate.

While this argument may logically from a skeptical viewpoint make perfect sense, in my experience as a working medium I know that different people bring different types of energy into the sessions that I do. Sympathetic, harmonious energies create a strong psychic vibration that allows me to easily connect with the communicating spirits, who, operating under such conditions are able to provide highly detailed, evidential information.

People who are closed off and negative for any reason, which would include hardcore skeptics, are exceptionally more difficult to work with as the energies are not as strong, the links with the spirit world weaker, and the connections more incomplete and vague. The ability of a person to place the information through subjective validation or otherwise is secondary to the main point that disharmonious conditions directly affect the delicate connections that allow for smooth and accurate telepathic communications from the spirit world to take place.

Skeptics and disbelievers should not be considered adversarial, but should be respected for their invaluable service of challenging the validity of spirit communication. Hardcore skeptics, despite their dogmatism, are generally intelligent, well-meaning individuals whose criticisms rightly address the inherent weaknesses of mediumistic communication. Mediums need to understand the skeptical position and raise their own standard of mediumship to the highest possible level.

List of Exercises

Acknowledgements

I am extremely grateful for the editing work done by Lisa Lemp Cheney and the awesome cover design and interior layout by my friend Greg Golem. I also thank my dear friend Juliana Beasley, a world famous photographer, for the headshot she took of me in the woods behind Etna Spiritualist Camp in Maine. I also want to thank my many students and friends for their love and support in getting this book out.

Resources

Mediumship Training Programs

National Spiritualist Association of Churches
www.nsac.org

Cassadaga Spiritualist Camp
www.cassadaga.org

Lily Dale Assembly
www.lilydaleassembly.com

Harmony Grove Spiritualist Association
www.harmonygrovespiritualist.org

Temple Heights Spiritualist Camp
www.templeheightscamp.org

Etna Spiritualist Association
www.campetna.com

Indiana Association of Spiritualists
Camp Chesterfield
www.campchesterfield.net

The Arthur Findlay College
www.arthurfindlaycollege.org

Mediumship Mastery Training Program
www.stevehermannmedium.com

Resources

Recommended Mediumship Development Books

Edwards, Harry, *A Guide for the Development of Mediumship,* Oxshott, UK, Spiritual Truth Press, 1998.

Leaf, Horace, *What Mediumship is: A Practical Treatise on How to Develop Mediumship,* London, UK, Psychic Press, 1938.

Nohavec, Janet and Giessmann, Suzanne, *Where Two Worlds Meet,* Chula Vista, California, Aventine Press, 2011.

Roberts, Ursula, *Hints on Mediumistic Development,* London, UK, Psychic Press, 1987.

Xavier, Francisco Candido and Luiz, Andre, *In the Domain of Mediumship,* Brasilia, Brazil, International Spiritist Council, 2006.

Wallis, E. W. and M. H., *A Guide to Mediumship, and Psychical Unfoldment; in Three Parts,* Various Publishers, 1898.

About the Author

Highly acclaimed for his detailed and accurate mediumship, Reverend Stephen Hermann is a world famous medium with incredible talent. A graduate of the experimental Hampshire College (Amherst, Massachusetts) for high achievers, Stephen is steeped in the history and philosophy of yoga, metaphysics and Spiritualism. Stephen holds credentials as an ordained minister, certified medium, and teacher with the National Spiritualist Association of Churches (USA), and has taught for the International Spiritualist Federation (UK).

A featured personality on television and radio worldwide, Stephen's mediumship has been documented by the Associated Press and other news media. A former research medium for the University of Virginia, he travels extensively teaching and demonstrating spirit communication and healing.

www.stevehermannmedium.com

Printed in Great Britain
by Amazon

41061514R00136